# ANSEO

# ANSEO

Úna-Minh Kavanagh

NEW ISLAND

ANSEO
First Published in 2019 by
New Island Books
16 Priory Office Park
Stillorgan
County Dublin
Republic of Ireland
www.newisland.ie

Print ISBN: 978-1-84840-749-7
eBook ISBN: 978-1-84840-750-3

Page from *Tomás agus Eithne á nGléasadh Féin* by Gunilla Wolde
(1980) reproduced by kind permission of An Gúm.
Typeset by JVR Creative India
Cover design by Anna Morrison, www.annamorrison.com
Printed by Scandbook, Sweden

New Island Books is a member of Publishing Ireland.

*To my mom, Noreen, my godmother, Maria,
and my partner, Pádhraic.*

*And in memory of my grandad, Paddy Kavanagh.*

# A Note on Language

Throughout this book, I have used Munster Irish as it is my native dialect. In my own texts and tweets that were originally published elsewhere, I have corrected typos and grammatical errors where appropriate. In texts and tweets by others, I have not corrected them here, reproducing them exactly as they were originally published, online or otherwise. Any other kinds of errors or oversights are entirely my responsibility.

# Contents

Cé Thusa? Where It All Began                    1

'Does She Speak English?'                       20

The Kingdom                                     39

Paddy Kavanagh, 1915–2006                       55

The Big Smoke                                   66

'Where Are You Really From?'                    86

From Pastimes to Full-time                     112

#WeAreIrish                                     125

Better Than One                                143

#FrásaAnLae                                    161

Tír Gan Teanga Tír Gan Anam                    168

Gaeilge is Your Superpower                     177

Paddy Kavanagh: An Appreciation               184

Acknowledgements                              186

# Cé Thusa? Where It All Began

How on earth did a little Asian girl become a proud Kerrywoman, thick accent and all? Shure look. It just so happens that another Kerrywoman chose Vietnam to search for a child to raise as her own in The Kingdom.

*Is fíor sin*, this is my truth: I don't have that red-haired, freckled, pale-skinned look that tourists think of when they read about Ireland. I have black hair, dark brown eyes that curve like a cat and light brown skin. That's right, I am a brown Irish girl! And if you saw me walking down an O'Connell Street anywhere in the country, you might, at a glance, take me for a tourist or, better still, an immigrant who has settled in Ireland.

It's true, I wasn't born here. In fact, I wasn't born anywhere near here. My story actually begins on the 4 July 1991, more than 10,000km from Ireland. I was born in the city of Hanoi, the capital of Vietnam. The first part of my first name 'Úna-Minh' (pronounced 'Oona-Ming') combines the Irish version of my grandmother's name, Winifred, with a play on the Irish word 'uan', meaning 'lamb'. The second part of my first name celebrates my Vietnamese heritage: 'Minh' is Sino-Vietnamese and means 'bright'. I am the only person in the world with the name Úna-Minh. Let's face it, I am not your usual Irishwoman.

I know very little about my Vietnamese birth family. Over the years, the information about them that has come my way has been sparse and impossible to verify. In the parts of my Vietnamese birth certificate where my birth parents' names should be, I find the words 'no father' and 'no mother'. My sense of how I came to be derives from the accounts of others (Mom, the doctors and officials in the hospital where I was born) and so I treat everything I've been told as a potential truth in my story.

What my mom, Noreen, knows is that my birth mother was much too poor and too young to look after me. She came from a village outside of Hanoi and when she was pregnant with me she was unmarried. Being single and pregnant brought great shame upon her family so there was never any question of her keeping me, her first daughter. It is not lost on me the similarity in how my birth mother was treated and the generations of Irish women and girls who suffered shame and stigma in their own families and communities.

While she was pregnant, to avoid rumours, my birth mother and her own mother moved from their small village to Hanoi, a huge city with a population of over a million people. It was an enormous step for them to take. They worked together in a factory along the Red River Delta making red bricks. I often wonder what it was like for my birth mother to leave everything behind and work in a city so different to her home village, just to save face. Heavily pregnant in Hanoi's stifling heat, she would have mixed the red clay into rectangular shapes and, as the bricks hardened, she would have carried them from one section of the factory to the other. Automated machinery had yet to come into use. The humidity in Vietnam, especially in the city, would make you swim in sweat. But Vietnamese women tend to wear long sleeves everywhere, to keep their skin as pale as possible (historically, browner skin suggested working in fields and, therefore, poverty). So not only would my birth mother have been pulling her pregnant body from one place to the other, but her arms would have been fully covered and she would have had no relief from the sweltering sun.

My mom has told me that my birth mother really didn't want to leave me when I was born, but she lived in a society where keeping up appearances was important regardless of your socio-economic status.

In Vietnam, the life of a woman was set in stone: you worked hard, found a prospective husband, married him quickly and then, just as quickly, had children who would grow up to take care of you when you were older. For those living in poorer communities, marriages were often used to create alliances between two families with a dowry. But for a woman in my birth mother's situation, with no man or even the promise of marriage – a woman with a fatherless child – no other man would ever want to marry her.

Two days after I was born, my birth mother returned to visit me. She wanted to keep me but couldn't and it would be the last time she saw me. It's the first difficult moment in my life that would shape my future irrevocably.

In 1989, Noreen Kavanagh was a schoolteacher from Tralee in her early forties working in Toronto. She was unmarried and for a few years had been thinking about having a baby. She was getting older and even though she wasn't in a serious relationship, she really wanted to be a mother. When she thought about her options for becoming a parent on her own, adoption made the most sense: she firmly believed that there were already so many children in the world who needed a loving and safe home. Besides, she wanted a daughter or a son, not a replica of herself!

*The pursuit of happiness*
**Tóraíocht an tsonais**

A neighbour of my mother's, Jacqueline, who was also from Tralee, had been living in Hanoi and working with UNICEF for two years. Jacqueline was also a single woman who had adopted two Vietnamese girls. My mom would listen, fascinated and full of admiration, to Jacqueline's stories about the adoption process and how her family came to be. And when Jacqueline and her daughters came home on visits to Ireland in the eighties, Mom loved spending time with them. So, it was from Jacqueline that my mother found the courage and inspiration to start looking at adopting a child from Vietnam.

Mom's teaching job in Tralee was secure enough to enable her to offer a caring home to a child. But she felt she just didn't have the time to pursue an adoption. She tells me now if she had stayed in Tralee she would not have gone to Vietnam and I wouldn't be writing this! In 1989 she had moved to Canada to work as a teacher in Toronto for two years. Her brother Dan had been living there for some years and he sponsored her move, which allowed her to work in Canada. After such an epic and brave journey across the ocean, and along with the excitement of the new opportunities this brought, her thoughts about adopting on her own were influenced by her new home. She had moved from an Irish town with a population of 17,000 to a thriving multicultural city of two million where she experienced very little ageism. When I ask her what this meant to her, she says that as a woman in her forties in Ireland she was expected to be well into a marriage and family by then. And because she had neither of her own, at home she was treated as 'old'. But in Canada, she felt no such pressure or discrimination and she marvelled at how relaxed Canadians were about individual life choices. If you were seventy or eighty you could do whatever you wanted – you could go ice skating and no one would care what age you were or what you looked like doing it. You could adopt a baby on your own in your forties and people would support you.

Mom came home to Ireland a few times during her time in Canada and each time she met up again with Jacqueline the desire to adopt grew ever stronger. On one such trip home, she made a conscious decision to bring important documents, like work references, back to Toronto. She had begun the earliest kind of preparation to become a parent and finally, after years of contemplating it, the exhilarating process of adoption from Vietnam was in motion. It was now or never! She decided if her application to adopt was unsuccessful she would chalk it all down as a chance to visit a new country and experience its culture. But she also decided that if she succeeded in adopting a baby in Vietnam, she would be returning to Ireland and not Canada.

Toronto was an attractive place to live, diverse, liberal and exciting, but Mom knew she would never be able to afford a house there, and living in an apartment with a newborn just was not for her. Though she was earning a good salary, the cost of living in Canada at that time was high; the house with a garden that she dreamed about was definitely off the cards. Family and home turf, the mountains and the sea were calling her back to Ireland.

Before she could travel to Hanoi, Mom had to get her paperwork in order. Her brother Dan's partner, Ellen, was a lawyer in Toronto and introduced Mom to the wonderful world of couriers; something she had never needed before in her life. Mom was unable to type but Ellen helped her to put together professional documents like statements of character, a letter of introduction and work references that showed Mom as a potential and capable adopter. Ellen's senior position within her law firm also meant that she had access to international shipping services and could liaise with Jaqueline on the Vietnam side of things when needed. One of the more impressive character references my mom included in her application was from the former Tánaiste and Minister for Foreign Affairs, Dick Spring. He was a fellow Tralee native and a neighbour of my mother and grandfather. He knew our family well, and they respected him and his late sister, Maeve, as people of integrity. Little did my mom know then, that a few years later she would meet him again, this time at an event in a bookstore in Tralee. I was very small, maybe three or four years old, very busy browsing the shelves of the children's section. Mr Spring approached me and began to chat to me about this and that. I don't think I could have replied at that age anyway, but Mr Spring also noticed that I seemed unable to hold his gaze. He said to me firmly and kindly, 'Always make eye contact when you are conversing with a person'. Well, the look on my face was forever captured in a photograph taken by my mother that lives in our family album, a reminder of his advice that has stayed with me to this day. Our family has a lot to thank him for.

Finally, the time had come to leave Toronto for Hanoi. Mom flew from Toronto to Detroit, Detroit to Tokyo and then Tokyo to Bangkok, spending nearly twenty-four hours on planes and in airports. Happily, somewhere along the way she was upgraded to executive class, she can't remember how or why, but it made her feel very fancy indeed. She arrived late at night in Thailand and took a short break to organise her visa before heading into Vietnam.

> The longest journey in life starts
> with one step
> **An turas is faide sa saol**
> **tosnaíonn sé le coiscéim amháin**

And as chaotic as the journey to Bangkok was, her brother Dan managed to get a message of encouragement to her at her hotel. It was an incredible boost of love to receive at just the right moment, having travelled all that way on her own. Later, she met an American who knew her way around and she recommended a Thai massage that would iron out the tension of the long-haul flights. Mom still swears by a Thai massage after a whole day's travelling.

From Bangkok, my mother sent her documents to Jacqueline in Vietnam, who had everything translated and notarised in advance of Mom's imminent arrival.

Nguyet, an interpreter who had helped Jacqueline during the adoption of her own daughters, also worked as my mother's official translator. Mom felt lucky to have Nguyet by her side as this honest and caring woman was able to deal with government officials and the incomprehensible and intimidating Vietnamese bureaucracy. Some days the roads would be shut down without any explanation; other days random police checks required Mom to have all of her identification on hand. With Nguyet never far away, she was ready for action and prepared to rearrange travel plans on a whim.

In the early nineties, Vietnam's economy and population was on the rise. But it certainly wasn't the bustling tourist destination it has since become. Poverty was everywhere, and for visitors it was still a war-stricken country. The tension between north and south Vietnam, the American War (1955–75) and other conflicts in the years since had moulded Hanoians into a stoic people, a disposition which is written across their faces. Poor infrastructure also meant Vietnam was considered a 'third world country'. The Red River Delta was less fertile than the southern Mekong Delta and food poverty was omnipresent in Hanoi and its surrounding areas.

The Red River Delta was the country's most densely populated region with millions of inhabitants crowded into the area. It has undergone substantial demographic growth since the fifties, the population rising from 6.5 million to around 14 million today. Constantly used by rice farmers, the river's resources were always in high demand. Despite the thriving farming industry, the excessive population growth led to a very low standard of living for the city's residents. Life was tough in Hanoi.

In the mid-nineties, Vietnam was one of the countries with the highest rates of adoption (along with China, South Korea and Russia). Unfortunately, later in the decade, there were numerous reports that babies were being bought or kidnapped away from their birth families. Some women were even being paid to become pregnant. In a poor country like Vietnam, adoption had become a lucrative business. Some of the shady business involved the US, Canada and Ireland. In the aftermath of these scandals, Vietnam closed down its adoption service for a few years. By 2005, however, Belgium, Canada, Denmark, France, Italy, Ireland, Sweden and the US had begun adopting from Vietnam again.

On only her second day in Vietnam, Mom was taken by Nguyet to one of the local hospitals, Bach Mai, where its director told her a baby born three days previously was available for adoption and would soon be moved to an orphanage if no adopter was found. That baby was me.

> *Her heart swelled with joy*
> **Líon a croí le háthas**

Built in 1911 during French colonial rule, Bach Mai Hospital is now one of the largest and most successful in Vietnam. It is a multi-field medical facility in Hanoi specialising in internal medicine. It was bombed during the American War; twenty-eight hospital staff were killed and almost the entire building was destroyed. As a single, white woman from an apparently affluent country, my mom was welcomed by the staff of Bach Mai Hospital. In a social a system where children worked and looked after their elders, they simply presumed my mother was securing her own future. From the paperwork Nguyet had provided the hospital with in advance, they knew she was well-educated and could provide a good home to a child. They just didn't want to send another child to an orphanage.

And so my mom saw me for the first time when I was just three days old – just one day after my birth mother had seen me for the last time. She couldn't get over how small I looked, how aware I seemed and how it felt to hold me close. My fingers wrapped easily around one of hers and I was looking up at her with curious brown eyes. A kind nurse took pictures of this fleeting moment. I had – and the photographic evidence is now here for all to see – a fine head of hair on me. She still believes it is an amazing and beautiful coincidence that we were in that hospital at the same time on the same day in 1991. In a city of 7.5 million people, we found each other and she promised to never let me go.

> *Life can hold many surprises*
> **Is iomaí cor sa saol**

> *This was worth waiting for*
> **B'fhiú fanacht leis seo**

The formal adoption process began immediately. While she waited for the papers to go through, Mom was supported by Pepita, another Irish woman who had also adopted two Vietnamese children. Pepita and Jacqueline, two incredible women, gave her practical and emotional support in a strange country. Pepita, who worked with the World Health Organisation (WHO) and the World Food Programme (WFP), had lived in Vietnam for almost a decade. She shared with Mom the cot and toys that her little girls no longer needed. She also knew where to buy baby formula in the Old Quarter of Hanoi and where to buy nice, soft baby clothes. Her meals are still remembered by my mother. Feeling overwhelmed by the paperwork, she came back one day to a roast beef feast which transported her immediately back to her own childhood in Kerry. It was these kindnesses that made all the difference to my mom, who at times felt daunted in a foreign country where she didn't speak the language.

When I was just twelve days old a compassionate consultant in the hospital suggested Mom take me to the apartment she was sharing with Jacqueline and her daughters. As the hospital was very busy – at times the nurses had little time to bottle feed – this consultant was concerned I wouldn't get the attention I needed. Jacqueline lived in a gated compound in a place called Vạn Phúc, south west of the city, where many foreign nationals working for organisations like UNICEF were living at the time. Armed guards enabled the government to observe the movement of foreigners within. It was a hot and sticky time in Hanoi that July with the temperature soaring into the thirties and so Mom would have to wait inside for hours for the day to cool before she could bring me out for air. On days when Mom was too tired to carry me around Vạn Phúc, Jacqueline's housekeeper, Madame Nga, would take me around the compound; she could handle the humidity. Madame Nga was fascinated to see the differences in baby care between her traditions and my new Western mother's. She was astonished when Mom put me over her shoulder, tapping my back to wind me after feeding. The Vietnamese encourage good digestion in babies by massaging the legs, back and body. Madame Nga would proclaim this method 'much better'. My mom found it hard to argue with her.

It felt like a lifetime to get the adoption paperwork signed off in Hanoi but, in fact, it was only five weeks. She couldn't help the niggling feeling that it might not work out, as she could never let herself be sure. There are no similarities between Vietnamese and the Irish, English, French and Spanish that Mom speaks, and she was left constantly wondering what was being said about her when she was in the room. When someone looked concerned while staring at a document, she became worried and Nguyet would do her best to explain what was going on. But she regularly found it stressful to rely on someone else's words to understand the complex adoption process and guide her through the miles of documentation. When she tells me now about all that she overcame I can't help but be in awe and admiration of her strength to get through it. It's clear that she's a well-capable woman!

At long last, my adoption was approved and my mom switched her focus to moving back to Ireland with her new baby daughter. She planned to leave with Pepita, but because the Vietnamese government monitored all foreigners' movements, it had to be informed when they wanted to leave Vietnam. In addition, I needed a passport! Wrapped up like a little burrito on the back of Nguyet's motorbike, I was carried to the office of a professional photographer. With my hair stuck up like a troll's and tiny wrinkly fingers, I look delightfully dumbstruck in my first passport photo.

Mom had left most of what she owned in Canada, giving much away to friends before she had left for Vietnam. She wanted to start afresh again with new things back in Ireland. What did come back with her were the many gifts she received from the staff of Bach Mai Hospital. The director gave her a decorative plate, which I still have. Others gave her silver baby bracelets to 'ward off bad spirits', silk clothes and hand-embroidered tablecloths. All things that would remind her of Vietnam in the years to come.

Five weeks after I was born I was wrapped in another blanket, sleeping in a basinet, flying to my new home in Ireland. When I talk to Mom about this moment, she can't help but get emotional. It was hard to believe that she had arrived in a foreign country filled with so much hope and weeks later was flying home with a child of her own. At Heathrow airport she stepped aside while immigration officials checked that everything was in order. Her heart pounded in her chest in case something was amiss. But she got the all clear and was soon on the home stretch to Ireland.

*I was giddy with relief*
**Bhí mearbhall orm le faoiseamh**

Maria, a close friend and former colleague of my mother's, who would become my loving godmother, met us in Dublin Airport and soon sent us on our way to my new hometown of Tralee. My grandad, Paddy Kavanagh, who was seventy-five at the time, welcomed us on our arrival back to Kerry. When I ask her how Grandad felt about me, Mom says he took the role of 'grandfather' very seriously and gave his heart and soul to it. He wanted to be involved as much as possible in our lives and help whenever he could.

Home sweet home
**Níl aon tinteán mar do thinteán féin**

Upon returning to Ireland, Mom took adoptive leave from her teaching job in Tralee (as a teacher she had been able to take a temporary career break from her Irish job to live and work in Canada for a couple of years), so she was finally able to spend uninterrupted time with me while settling back into home. My grandfather's support was precious during those early days and weeks. In 1991, Tralee was much more homogenous than it is now and to her old neighbours, Mom looked a bit suspicious. Tongues were wagging. Why had this woman gone on a career break for two years and returned with an Asian baby?

Never mind the gossips
**Ná bac le lucht na cúlchainte**

But the Tralee locals' curiosity and tongue wagging were of little interest to my mom and my grandad. They welcomed me into their home and into both of their huge hearts. And it's true to say that it was from those first days that the Irish language welcomed me and has never let me go. I was a brown Irish girl growing up in a single-parent family, and I was to become an extremely proud Kerrywoman.

> *Walk tall and be proud of yourself*
> **Seas suas agus bíodh mórtas ort asat féin**

# 'Does She Speak English?'

When Mom brought me home to Ireland to live with herself and Grandad in Tralee, they had no idea what kind of life would be ahead of me. But I had a fantastic childhood, thanks to their love and support. By the time I arrived, my grandad had retired from An Garda Síochána so he had loads of time for me. He was a *cainteoir dúchais* (native Irish speaker) who spoke Irish from the cradle and his love of the language trickled into my consciousness almost immediately. His influence never felt forced or like a chore.

The new grandaughter of the famous storyteller and retired Garda Kavanagh instantly became a talking point both within and outside of our family. He was a traditional, fuss-free Irishman so no doubt they wondered what my story was. There were looks of awe around Tralee as he was spotted wheeling this small Asian baby in her buggy and he speaking *as Gaeilge* to her. I was an 'exotic' new addition to the town. There was even an article in the local newspaper about me; there's no better way to know you're the talk of the town than an appearance in *Kerry's Eye*! As he walked around town with me, 'Does she speak English?' became a regular inquiry. And he would declare to anyone who would actually listen, 'Ní hamháin Béarla, ach Gaelainn, ambaiste' (Not only English but Irish, indeed). He volunteered this information even when it might seem like no one was taking any notice, satisfying only their own curiosity with the question. More on these 'innocent' kinds of questions later.

> A swell of pride
> **Taom mórtais**

Time and time again he would have to explain our situation and though it must have been exhausting, he never let his pride in me falter. There was even one time when Grandad had me out in the buggy in downtown Tralee and a woman came up to him, saying in all seriousness:

'Oh Paddy, what will you do when she grows up and starts speaking Vietnamese? You won't be able to understand her.'

Well, I snorted my tea right out of my nose the first time Mom told me that story. I would love to have seen Grandad trying to maintain his composure.

He never rolled his eyes, but he could give a deadpan stare that would rattle a snake.

*Ignorance is bliss*
**Seachnaíonn súil ní nach bhfeiceann**

But like so many children who are loved, I didn't notice how precious and finite my time with my grandad would be. 'Labhair Gaelainn liom, a chailín' (Speak Irish to me, girleen), he would say to me, and I, in my thick Kerry-shtyle accent, would talk back to him in English. I loved to act the playful pup and he knew it. Since his death in my teens, there have been countless times that I wish I could have spoken in Irish with him again, even just for a few minutes. Writing this book, I am reminded of the many questions that I would love to ask him about his life, questions that never even occurred to me as a child.

*Childhood innocence*
**Soineantacht na hóige**

When I was very small, Mom worked as a *múinteoir* (teacher) in one of Tralee's local primary schools and I attended a Gaelscoil up the road from our family home in St Brendan's Park, a housing estate in town. The decision that I would attend a Gaelscoil was an obvious one and by going to a different one to her own, Mom hoped I could avoid the pressure of being a teacher's daughter. She also wanted me to have the freedom that some distance would give me. Throughout my primary education, I was the only brown child in my school. I was also the only 'foreign' child in my class. Mind you, not that I noticed, as I was much more interested in play dough than what people were saying about me. It was only towards the end of my primary school years that my peers began to make sly 'slanty eyes' remarks or slipped in words like 'ching chong' at the end of their digs. I didn't understand why and was deeply hurt. For years there had never been an issue and all of a sudden, this? We were in the same class, I could speak and write in Irish just as well as they could, I didn't mock them, and my mother and grandad were white like theirs – I just couldn't grasp why I was part of a 'joke'.

Eventually, this bullying had got so bad that I was very down and didn't want to go to school anymore. And I adored school! Even at a young age, not yet ten years old, I managed to open up to my mother.

Her reaction was immediate, and I felt safe knowing that she was rooting for me. She marched up from her school to my school to put an end to it, once and for all. And she did so with compassion and reason. She met with the principal and explained how I was feeling and how it was affecting my progress. The bullying ended and I was so relieved.

> *The unacceptability of bullying*
> **Ní raibh aon ghlacadh le bulaíocht**

The relief of not having to deal with any more bullies brought me back to the happy child I had been. I was back to being a 'normal' child again, playing games like *Gardaí 'gus Gadaí* (Cops and Robbers) in the school yard without fear. When Grandad would walk me to school, we would always be late, strolling and chatting *as Gaeilge*, so that I often missed the roll call in the school yard ('Anseo!'). After many a 'tá brón orm' (I'm sorry), the teachers accepted my absolutely valid excuse of 'Bhíos ar siúlóid le mo sheanathair' (I was on a walk with my grandad). We marvelled that we got away with it for so long. And I remember those walks as truly some of the best moments of my young life.

*Why is it that you are
always late?*
**Canathaobh a mbíonn tú
i gcónaí déanach?**

Despite our tardiness, education was very important to my grandad. Much like his immense pride
in our Kerry GAA team, he was also very proud of
speaking *Gaelainn na Mumhan* (Munster Irish; note
that 'Gaelainn' is Kerry-Irish for 'Gaeilge'). So, I
know where I got my loyalty and ambition for learning from. While I was fortunate to be able to go
into education with ease and live well throughout
my childhood, my grandad had a very different and
much tougher upbringing in the early-1920s.

Paddy Kavanagh was born in 1915 in Baile na nGall,
a small fishing village about fifty kilometres from
Tralee and one of Kerry's many *Gaeltachtaí*. He was
in school in west Kerry until he was about fourteen
years old and, apart from that, stayed at home growing potatoes and sodding the turf. He was one of
eight children and it was a struggle to survive. He left

to join the De La Salle Brothers in County Laois with the intention of becoming a brother himself. At the time, for people like his parents – a fisherman and a housewife – this was a great opportunity for an education. The only viable alternative was emigration to England or the US.

In 1934, when he was nineteen years old and still at De La Salle, Grandad received a letter from his parents saying one of his brothers, Michael, had had a nervous breakdown and was in St Finan's mental hospital in Killarney. This was a dreaded place in those days, somewhere very few people left. The letter was marked 'personal' but the De La Salle Brothers intercepted it and Grandad was sent packing. It was shameful to have a family member who was mentally unstable, something the brothers didn't want publicly known. They didn't give him enough money to get home to Baile na nGall and he got stuck in Tralee. Some kindly stranger gave him lodgings for a night, and he managed to hitch a lift further west the following day.

Later that same year, he completed his exams for the Gardaí in English and was recruited in 1935. He trained for six months in the Garda Depot in Dublin. His first station was Glenbeigh and he stayed there for over fourteen years. The bicycle was his only means of transport, 'the poor man's Mercedes', he called it, and he adored it.

Glenbeigh was a small quiet town where life was uncomplicated. With just a church, shop and Garda station, it was the epitome of simple Irish living. While he was assigned to the Glenbeigh beat in 1936, he met my grandmother, Winnie, who was from Flagmount, County Clare, and working as a district nurse. My grandmother wasn't a native Irish speaker but that didn't stop him falling head over heels for her. He always described Winnie as his 'first and last love'. They would go on to have four children while living in Glenbeigh. Sadly she died of a blood clot following a foot operation in Cork in 1979, just one year after my grandad had retired. Their dream of relaxing and travelling together died with her. He never remarried after her death. Obviously, I never met her and we don't have many photos of her, but whenever I do come across one, I am taken aback by how much my mom looks like her. Years of compassion from working as a district nurse are there in her features. She has a twinkle in her eyes, a beautiful smile, soft white hair just like my mom's hair now and I know in my heart I would have loved her as much as I loved my grandad.

He used to tell us that in all his time in Glenbeigh, he could recall only one crime: the poor box in the church was once broken into, an event he reckoned was due to the poverty and hunger of the time. Glenbeigh's small community supported each other where they could and it didn't become the tourism hotspot we know now until many decades later. Rather, it was a place you would pass through on your way to someplace else and its people often struggled to make a living from the surrounding land.

When they moved to Tralee, cycling remained Grandad's only mode of transport; he never learned to drive. He travelled miles and miles on his bicycle, often to and from the bog near Raemore where he would cut turf. Any hour he could spare from his work he would slip away to the bog, pipe in his pocket. It was there he would meet friends from the Gaeltacht, out in the fresh air, and they would converse and reminisce in Irish about their childhoods. He lived for the simple life, where himself, his family, his bicycle, his friends and his pipe were all he needed for entertainment.

> *To lead a simple life*
> **Saol simplí a chaitheamh**

Living in Tralee he only had limited interactions with the Irish language, but as infrequent as they were, he cherished them. In particular, it was his friendship with one Johnín Phil O'Sullivan that brought him con-siderable joy. Johnín lived in 'The Bungalows' behind our house. He too was a native Irish speaker, from Baile an Sceilg on the next headland south of Daingean Uí Chúis. As though on a mission, Johnín always donned a *caipín* (a traditional peaked cap) and carried a walking stick for his strolls around our housing estate. My former primary school teacher, Máistir Colm, told us that Johnín made great use of the free travel in his later years. He'd catch the bus 'back west' to the Gaeltacht in Dún Chaoin, out and about for the day and enjoyed a pint or two before coming home. His is just one of the many warm, kind faces I can recall from my childhood. Much like my grandfather, Johnín was a man content in his own company. Whenever he spotted my grandad outside our house, pruning roses or masterfully yanking out weeds, Johnín would be straight out to chat to him. And to see these two men together was to witness a rare and special exchange in the Irish language and to know that speaking *as Gaeilge* meant an awful lot to them.

My grandad had a long career with the Gardaí in Kerry and even when he went to work in Tralee in 1949, it was mostly a quiet time. I suppose he became best known locally for his involvement with the Maurice 'Moss' Moore case in Raemore in November 1958, the true story that inspired John B. Keane's play, *The Field*. Moss Moore and his neighbour, Dan Foley, were at loggerheads over land rights and while their legal case was pending, Moore went missing, his body found some ten days later just twenty yards from his home. Of course, suspicion rested immediately on Foley who would deny the murder to the end of his days. No one was ever charged for Moore's death and it became one of the greatest unsolved Irish murders of the twentieth century. As one of the Gardaí who knew both men, my grandfather was deeply acquainted with the details of the case. He used to sod the turf with both men and was particularly fond of Moss.

The night before his famed death, Moss had called the Garda station asking for my grandad to call out to his house because Dan was disturbing him. He said he would when he could, but between one thing and another, a few days went by. Many years later, he told me this was one of his greatest regrets in life.

The real-life events that Grandad experienced and the stories he told about them nourished his gift of the gab. He was one of those rare people who captivated those around him with his storytelling. Mom used to tell me 'you would stand in a field in the rain just to hear him speak'. He always nabbed the opportunity to raise a glass for a singsong in the pub (much to my regular embarrassment). He couldn't wait to belt out 'The Rattlin' Bog' at an Irish wedding, and he loved to encourage others to join in on a tune. That was Paddy Kavanagh, my grandad.

> *The night ended with a sing-song*
> **Cuireadh clabhsúr ar an oíche le babhta amhránaíochta**

> *I love the plop of whiskey into a glass*
> **Is breá liom fuisce ag doirteadh de phlab isteach i ngloine**

I always wonder how difficult it was for him to switch from Irish to English. English was useful to him in furthering his career and in supporting his family, but the decision to take his Garda exams and to work in English was made with his head, not with his heart. In his downtime, Grandad was an avid reader with his own personal library of books in English and Irish in our family home in Tralee. We called it a 'library' but it was, in all honesty, a coat room. That small room with its shelves towering over me, overflowing with books, filled me with wonder every time I entered it. And though he read and enjoyed an array of English-language books, he always returned to his Irish, nabbing every opportunity to bring it back into our home. Seeing it in print or hearing it on the radio would transport him back to his days in the Gaeltacht. He wasn't afraid to correct people when he spotted a spelling or grammatical mistake in the Irish language, but never in a way that would embarrass or rebuke. Even in highlighting an error, my grandad was a gentleman.

So, as a child, I often found marks in my Irish-language storybooks, correcting the standard Irish to *fíor-Ghaelainn Chiarraí* (real Kerry-Irish). Looking at them now I can't help but feel emotional when I see how beautiful his handwriting was. I'm instantly reminded of him with a pen in his hand. He wrote in a variation of the *seanchló* (old font) and his notes bring a wave of nostalgia anytime I see them. I'm in love with the dialectal variations in pronunciation and spelling in Irish. (There are three main dialectal regions in Ireland: Munster Irish which covers Kerry, Cork and Waterford; Conamara Irish in Galway and Ulster Irish in Donegal.) Even when I hear someone speaking a million miles a minute on the radio I get excited at their use of the words that I grew up with. My grandad would constantly joke with me that the Irish in Kerry had the best rhythm to it. These days we're encouraged to use the Caighdeán Oifigiúil (Official Standard) which is the Irish you see written in schoolbooks and in grammar books. But between all of the dialects' variations I think there's something really beautiful in how each region differs in their communication. To me it enhances our national language and demonstrates that, in Irish, just as there are in English, there are multiple ways to write and say something.

> *Grandad was full of mischief*
> **Bhí daideo lán le diabhlaíocht**

From my grandfather, I learned the West Munster dialect of the Irish language. Later, I discovered the more 'official' or common versions in grammar books. And later still, I encountered even more variations in East Munster, Conamara and Ulster Irish. Once, when I was at college in Dublin, I missed a lecture due to illness. The next day I told the lecturer that 'bhíos breoite' (I was sick). He cocked his head to one side, no idea what I was trying to say. I reddened; I was so sure I had the right word but it wasn't working so I switched to English. But it turns out 'breoite' is a Munster word and the standard version is 'tinn'. To make matters even more confusing, 'tinn' doesn't mean sick in Kerry-Irish, it means sore, so you can imagine what state I was in by the end of the class.

| West Munster Dialect | Common | English |
| --- | --- | --- |
| breoite | tinn | sick |
| Bhíos, cheapas, thugas srl. | Bhí mé, cheap mé, thug mé etc. | I was, I thought, I took |
| Gaelainn | Gaeilge | Irish |
| chí | feic | to see |
| tigh | teach | house |
| leis | freisin | as well |
| cairt | carr | car |
| Canathaobh? | Cén fáth? | Why |
| Conas tánn tú? | Conas atá tú? | How are you? |
| Dhein/ Dheineas | Rinne mé | I did |

With Grandad at home teaching me essential Kerry-Irish, at school I was also lucky to have teachers who inspired me to love the language. Every single one of my teachers, from baby infants right up to sixth class, were kind to me. Without blinking, they accepted that I was just like the others in my class, a child growing up with the Irish language. They didn't treat me differently and neither did I get any special attention. But there were two teachers who went above and beyond to instil in me confidence and whose enthusiasm and wisdom I still draw on as an adult speaker of Irish.

Máistir Colm taught me in fourth class and Máistir Caball taught me in fifth and sixth class. Máistir Caball was a local Tralee-man with grey hair and glasses who reminded me of Owl in *Winnie the Pooh*. I clung to his every word in class. He knew my grandad and I think of them as kindred spirits in their equal passion for storytelling and music. His enthusiasm was infectious, and I honestly couldn't wait to go to school to see him. To this day I can still play on the tin whistle the tune of 'Fáinne Geal an Lae' ('Dawning of the Day'), can sing 'Válsáil Mathilda' ('Waltzing Mathilda' ) in Irish and can recite, off by heart and *as Gaeilge*, stories like 'An Bradán Feasa' ('The Salmon of Knowledge') and 'Clann Lir' ('The Children of Lir'). I love that this was my start in life but the digital world I live in now thrives on stories of 280 characters on Twitter. Anyway, with Máistir Caball's help, our school band, in which I was a proud player of the *bosca ceoil* (piano accordion), won Tralee's coveted St Patrick's Day Parade Award several times. One for the CV!

Máistir Colm had a different kind of energy. A man from the Kerry Gaeltacht of Baile an Sceilg, he was, quite simply, a kind and generous man. His calm presence and fluency in the Irish language, just like my grandad's, resonated with me. He was patient with us, and never treated us like an annoyance. There was one day when his patience was especially noted. An RTÉ film crew visited our school in 2001. Mom was taking part in a television programme about foreign adoption into Ireland and I, by then ten years old, and another adopted boy were being featured. As you can imagine, there was great excitement in school, and everyone was on their best behaviour. I even got a new hairband for the occasion, which jazzed up my brown school uniform very nicely. Some of the footage was filmed in my classroom and I remember making art for the whole of that day. As the cameras zoomed in on my 'exotic' brown face, I was concentrating very hard with a stick of glue in my little hands. Poor Máistir Colm had to say the morning's roll call several times so that the film crew could get the 'perfect shot' and, in the end, he was just doodling on his book instead of actually ticking off names. There's really only so much craic to be had saying the same names over and over again. Like I say, he was a patient man. Thanks to the production team at RTÉ who sent them to us after the broadcast, we still have the tapes they recorded, as well as behind the scenes footage of Grandad teasing me about not speaking Irish to him all the time. There's also a scene of me drawing on my own face with Crayola markers. Classy!

Whenever Grandad gave me a new word at home, I couldn't wait to try it out in school. And whether I understood it or not, Máistir Colm often became my test subject. Once, Grandad had said I shouldn't leave Thomas the Tank Engine lying around or 'bheinn i dtrioblóid' (I'd be in trouble) with Mom later and so I, delighted at the sound of the new words, headed off to school to use them. (On reflection this probably wasn't Grandad's intention!) I distinctly remember Máistir Colm being on schoolyard duty as I ran around playing with my friends yelling jubilantly 'Táim i dtrioblóid! Táim i dtrioblóid!' (I'm in trouble!) Clearly onto me, Colm kindly remarked with a smile, 'Trioblóid? Ana-mhaith Úna-Minh.' (Trouble? Very good Úna-Minh!) My test was a roaring success.

> *You're only young once*
> **Ní thagann an óige fé**
> **dhó choíche**

The kindness of my teachers and the support and love of my mom and grandad ensured that I had a wonderful time growing up. I was allowed to be myself – creative, theatrical, funny and yes, quite stubborn too! Even though every so often there were those who took it upon themselves to call out my 'differences', I had, in all honesty, a very wholesome and normal Irish childhood. And I was enthralled by my grandad. Though I was in a single-parent household, I never felt any lack. He was my father figure, and an absolute hero of mine.

I spent the rest of my schooldays doing what any Irish child in the nineties did: playing tip the can, collecting hundreds of *Pokémon* cards, investing in a doomed Irish dancing career and being the worst footballer Kerry has ever seen. Why our local team put me in goal I'll never know. Let me tell you, Sam Maguire would have been mortified!

# The Kingdom

You can take this woman out of Kerry, but she'll always be a Kerrywoman. Even though I've lived in Dublin for nearly a decade and, mostly due to extortionate rents, I now live in County Louth, the southwest calls me home every year. I cannot compare the scenery and that fresh Atlantic air. And whenever someone comes to visit us in Ireland, I always point them to 'The Kingdom'. When I was a child, my mom always made sure that we travelled every inch of our county, but despite this – and apart from my obvious bias as a Kerrywoman – the Gaeltacht was and still is our first choice for holidays.

It was just the three of us in my family, and we were a tight-knit team. Grandad always spoke to me in Irish and my Mom, not a native speaker of Irish but close to the language nonetheless, would do the same in English. I was getting the best of both worlds! Depending on how I felt (or what I wanted from the adults) I could choose the sing-song Irish or the practical English to express myself. Either way, they understood me and both parts of my inner self were fed constantly. Even on my summer holidays from my Gaelscoil in Tralee, my mom made sure I got my daily dose of Irish. But while my beginnings with the Irish language were primarily with my Grandad, my mother's journey with the language had been quite different.

> *A close-knit family*
> **Teaghlach atá fite**
> **fuaite ina chéile**

My grandmother, Winnie, wasn't an Irish speaker. Though Grandad did speak a bit of Irish to my mother and her siblings, English was the dominant language in her home. In the mid-twentieth century, Irish was still considered a beautiful language but limiting in its use and application in contemporary Irish life. In my mother's childhood home, there was a shift towards using English more often. Not one of my mom's brothers or sister had any intention of using the Irish language in their careers and adult lives and so it was relegated to a second language. But my mother flourished at Irish in school. She just enjoyed it and she loved her father's connection with his family in the Gaeltacht. She fondly remembers visiting them in the fishing village of Baile na nGall and how they collected fresh crabs legs as they were unloaded by the fishermen onto the pier. With four children to put through school and university, my grandparents, like their parents before them, did everything in their power to help them fly the coup of the Ireland of the fifties and sixties. And so it was rare for my mother to see both parents at home at the same time. My grandmother began her night duty in Bon Secours Hospital in Tralee at 9 p.m. and worked until 9 a.m. the following morning. Mom would meet her mother coming home from work on her way to school. After a few hours rest, my grandmother would be up again at 2 p.m. to make bread and get ready for dinner. Grandad worked the beat in Tralee during the day and returned home after dinner.

*Childhood memories*
**Cuimhní na hóige**

Their family holidays were uncomplicated affairs and each time they returned west to the Gaeltacht, the familiarity and the language were even more welcoming than the year before. They did visit other parts of Kerry, including Baile an Lochaigh, at the foot of

Mount Brandon on the northern part of the Dingle Peninsula, where Mom's paternal grandmother came from. Here they visited her cousins, the Moriartys, and took long walks through the Com an Lochaigh valley. Her many cousins, especially Tony and Páid, and their large extended families, had magical Kerry-Irish like her own father. Their eyes would light up as they spoke it fluently; it was a kind of poetry and it made her feel at home.

> *We have uplifting*
> *memories of that time*
> **Tá cuimhní croíúla**
> **againn ón am sin**

My mom has a degree in Irish, philosophy and English from University College, Dublin (UCD). Later, she gained a distinction in teaching from Trinity College Dublin, and a diploma in education from Mary Immaculate College, Limerick. She tells me that she chose Irish as one of her core subjects for two reasons, she thought it would be easy because she had grown up with Irish and she thought she'd be good at it. She soon discovered two things: a) It wasn't easy and b) She wasn't as good as she thought she was!

In UCD in the late sixties, exam results were posted on a wall for all to see (I'm so glad they abandoned that!) and if your name wasn't there, you had not passed. In 1972, in her final year, Mom was preparing to head to Papua New Guinea as part of her Voluntary Service Overseas (VSO). She had trained in advance of teaching abroad and she was excited to be leaving Ireland for a while to experience a completely different culture. All she needed to do was pass her exams.

The day had come, and the exam results went up on the walls. And as Mom waded through the crowd to get to the results notices, her worst fear came to be. Her name wasn't there. She was absolutely mortified. She realised she had been a little too arrogant about her ability in the Irish language and in that moment learned the hard lesson that she hadn't given it the study time it deserved. But in Kerry, her parents were delighted she hadn't passed because they saw it as a sign for her not to go abroad. The idea of teaching abroad was alien to them; sure, wasn't heading off to Papua New Guinea like going into space, risky and dangerous? They were truly worried that she would never come back from the other side of the world. But Mom thought differently. In her pure determination to get to Papua New Guinea and indeed some embarrassment over failing, she studied hard to re-sit her Irish exam and passed the second time around. Irish has been with her ever since.

Her ability to move past these kinds of failure, or 'blips' as she likes to call them, revealed itself strongest when she became a primary schoolteacher. By the time she returned from Papua New Guinea in the mid-seventies, she found the schoolchildren were once again open and receptive to learning the Irish language. And of all the subjects she had to teach, Irish became her favourite. She would go on to teach for over forty years.

Just as my mother had when she was a child, we three headed 'back wesht' every summer for nearly ten years. Going back west for us meant a summer in the Gaeltacht, sixty kilometres away from home, where the seaside would be a few minutes' drive from us and we would be surrounded by rolling green hills. Mom would pack the boot of the car with everything but the kitchen sink and we'd trundle out of Tralee in our old Opel Astra (#RestinPieces). With the paint peeling off the sides and the wheels sinking into the ground the car would be wheezing from the weight of everything in it. Our destination each year was Baile an Fheirtéaraigh (known locally as An Buailtín), a small village in the Kerry Gaeltacht. On a friend's recommendation, Mom had rented a holiday apartment owned by a charismatic woman named Eileen O'Shea, a Kerrywoman and *cainteoir dúchais*. She loved people to know that she was an Irish speaker and that she was happy to speak with them in her native tongue. We loved Baile an Fheirtéaraigh's easy approach to Irish living. Even coming from a town the size of Tralee, life seemed simpler there. With less than fifty inhabitants during the nineties, the village had just a few pubs, a local shop, a handful of houses, some places to eat, a church, a school and one of the village's proudest attractions: Músaem Chorca Dhuibhne in the old schoolhouse (which is a lot more than other Irish villages). On our summer holidays in the Gaeltacht, we wanted for nothing else.

> We headed off for a
> relaxing escape
> **D'imíomar linn faoi
> choinne sos suaimhneach**

Winding our way through the countryside, past the village of Camp and through the extreme twists and turns of An Chonair (Conor Pass), one of Ireland's highest mountain passes, we gazed across the corrie lakes and magnificent lush green valley of the Cloichearaí townland. Though An Chonair is a serpentine one-lane road best avoided in bad weather, it is also the most direct way to Daingean Uí Chúis and is just beautiful on a rare fine day. The road is so narrow it feels like squeezing through the eye of a needle and thunderous excitement would fill me knowing the potential for plummeting into the gorge at every sharp corner. The thrill of this was especially acute when Mom had to signal with her right hand to an oncoming car to shimmy in so we could pass by unscathed.

> *We had a taste for adventure*
> **Bhí dúil san eachtraíocht**
> **againn**

In Baile an Fheirtéaraigh, Eileen's home was tucked up a mossy pathway and hidden from the main road. At some point, she had built an extension onto it for guests, an apartment attached to her house with three small bedrooms, a bathroom and a kitchen. Eileen said it was perfect for her because if her guests were ever annoying her she could just retreat to her own quarters. We hoped her comment wasn't about us!

The apartment had the usual decorations seen in Irish homes from the 1960s onwards: a picture of US President John F. Kennedy along with the Sacred Heart in a bedroom. Despite its quirks, Eileen's apartment felt like a second home to me and I adored it. Eileen herself had a rich Kerry accent, whether speaking English or Irish. She could be hard to understand at times but she was always warm, funny and full of welcome.

Two of the bedrooms had twin beds while the third had its own double bed and was randomly equipped with a shower. As a young child, just eight years old, I had to clamber my way into the blue plastic base of this shower, barely able to lift my leg over the ledge and then somehow wash myself as the water sprayed horizontally out of the shower door straight onto the carpeted floor of the bedroom. You've all been there! And then, assuming the whole carpet was drowned anyway, we had our showers, one after the other, and let the carpet dry out as the day went by and we went gallivanting around the Kingdom. One of the other bedrooms had the only sink in the apartment, so we had to make a little detour from the stand-alone toilet. The third bedroom had a fireplace in one of its walls, which we never used. Mom used to joke that staying there felt like we were part of a living exhibition at the Guggenheim Museum it was so bizarre. And don't get me started on the electrics! Apart from the socket for the fridge, there was just one other electrical outlet in the kitchen and a three-pin round socket at that! We were totally flummoxed by this; even in the early nineties these sockets were archaic. The first time we saw it, Mom carted myself and Grandad off to Foxy

John's (Pub and Hardware) in Daingean Uí Chúis for an adapter and from then on, she never arrived in Baile an Fheirtéaraigh without an extension lead and that was that! Sure, there was a small chance of being electrocuted, but that was all part of the fun.

There was no television in our little apartment and that suited us just fine because surrounding us were green pathways and overgrown routes climbing the hill nearby. I'd wander down one path to get to my favourite run-down stone shack where a docile donkey waited for me. Later I wandered back to our apartment past the fuchsia, my legs tackled by heather, bracken and gorse.

> *It is not the good that was but the present good that matters*
> **Ní hé an mhaith a bhí ach an mhaith atá**

Grandad loved visiting Eileen's home. Not only were there more people to speak Irish with, but it brought him back to his beloved Gaeltacht. He'd have the paper out and his pipe in his mouth, and be sitting in front of Eileen's house and when I looked back at him every so often I would see little puffs of smoke around his handsome face. The birds would be singing in the hedges and brambles, and the sun would be splitting the stones. Having lived in Dublin city for many of the last ten years, I miss the Atlantic air. For me, nothing beats opening my door and seeing the sea and the mountains across the lands right in front of me. And though I was on my holidays in Baile an Fheirtéaraigh, I think of it now as home. These days it's a special treat to come back to Kerry for a break and I understand now how my grandad felt returning to the Gaeltacht with us.

> *Don't postpone joy*
> **Ná cuir an sonas ar athlá**

Each summer I pro-actively scouted the shop for Cornetto ice creams, sometimes a Loop the Loop ice-pop, a new multicoloured bucket, a fishing net and once, when I was feeling extra adventurous, a lilo. Yes, okay, it was entirely impractical for Irish summers when the Atlantic would freeze your arse off but to ten-year-old Úna-Minh it looked cool with flaming red streaks across it. I brought it out one summer and had a whale of a time for about fifteen minutes until I couldn't feel my toes in the water any longer. After that, it stayed in the garage for years until a mouse ate a hole in it.

> *You've been arsing about*
> *all summer*
> **Tá tú i do shuí ar do thóin**
> **an samhradh ar fad**

Some summers Mom improved her Irish on a teaching course in nearby Dún Chaoin, learning more about the Gaeltacht's storytellers and folklore. I tagged along on her excursions to important places like the Blasket Islands. When she took a break from her studying, we also drove across the Ring of Kerry several times, stopping at the unspoiled beaches of Wine Strand and Béal Bán, where I made sandcastles and forts soon destroyed by the sea. I am still mad for beaches and the ocean – I can't get enough of them – and Béal Bán is still one of the many glorious stretches of sand in Ireland which hasn't been overrun by visitors. Just a few minutes' drive down from our rented holiday apartment, its kilometre or so of sand made it a famous destination for pony racing. My great-grandad fished there, and my grandad raced his currach from Béal Bán to Baile na nGall across Smerwick Harbour.

> *Sun-baked beaches*
> **Tránna griandóite**

At night, Mom, Grandad and I headed to either one of the local pubs, Tigh Uí Chatháin or Tigh Peig, where the adults enjoyed many tipples and I drank Rock Shandy, sucked on Black Jacks and played pool. I claimed several high scores on Super Bubble Bobble (a mouthful, isn't it?), forever my badge of honour.

We visited Mom's cousins too, of course, many of whom still reside in the Kerry Gaeltacht and listening to them speak with the lilt in their voices always charmed me. Brought around the farmlands and households of the area, wearing my snazzy denim dungarees, Irish and Irishness was the thing that connected all of us, brought us closer on those summer days. The Irish sounded like music to me. My cousins' turns of phrase had a rhythm that I could never feel in the English I heard in Tralee. Like with the teachers in my Gaelscoil the rest of the year, I never felt like I was treated differently because of how I looked.

We sat in houses where the stove was the focal point, tea towels hanging above it and a *cupán tae* in our hands. There would be stories and, if Grandad had his way, a sing-song and every so often Mom would announce that I was an excellent tin whistle player and I should play a tune. I would feign embarrassment, of course, but I was a competent player and the tin whistle was whipped out in full force! 'Fáinne Geal an Lae' ('Dawning of the Day') was a standard with which Grandad serenaded us, his eyes closed, an *uisce beatha* in one hand and his other hand placed on his knee. He was a rare soul and a storyteller par excellence. The room would go quiet and after a while, following the stories and laments (as Irish songs tend to be), the adults would all join in with gusto for the last verse. I'd be up on my Grandad's lap or cross-legged on the floor, bewitched by these moments.

> *The memories are still alive*
> **Maireann na cuimhní fós**

So far, so normal an Irish childhood, right? When I was young, I never noticed how unusual I was to anyone around me. In my tiny immediate family and with the many cousins and extended family around Kerry and Dublin, acceptance was always the immediate reaction. I was doing exactly what they were doing, hopping on tractors, playing with ponies and speaking Irish. Apart from my skin colour, we weren't different in the slightest.

My healthy and personal relationship with the Irish language was of huge importance to my grandad and my mom and the summer weeks we spent 'back west' only made it stronger. It was a practical way for my grandfather to ensure that the memories of his own family wouldn't be lost, passed down in the stories that I tell you here.

> *It's hard to define Irishness*
> **Is deacair a rá cad is**
> **Éireannachas ann**

Even as a child, I appreciated every single moment I spent in the Gaeltacht. Like a lot of Irish people, my mother's cousins always felt like my first cousins, not extended family. Their resilience in a world where English was still being shoved into their lives filled me with admiration and determination to keep the language as a part of life. When my grandad passed away, we continued to visit the Gaeltacht every year, for it was his life, spirit and memory that was our *nasc* (connection) to the land.

Thinking back on it all now, I can appreciate just how unusual I must have been, this Asian-looking child swanning around Kerry with a white family, fluent in Irish and holidaying in the Gaeltacht. But all of this makes me appreciate my upbringing and has further established my strong Kerry loyalty and pride. My home was always full of love and adventure was right on my doorstep.

# Paddy Kavanagh, 1915–2006

It was my grandad's longing for the Gaeltacht that brought us back there so much. He could be like a dog pining to go home. With each visit back I could feel my bond with the Gaeltacht and with him grow stronger and more real. My Irish wasn't as strong as his native tongue, but I knew he loved every syllable I spoke of it. In my innocence, I thought he would be around to chat to forever.

In June 2006 I headed back west again but this time I was embarking on one of my first adventures with people my own age on a course at Irish College. Gaeltacht courses are held in the summer across Ireland's Irish-speaking regions like Corca Dhuibhne in County Kerry, Conamara on the west coast and in the midlands at Rath Cairn. For us teenagers it was an opportunity to make new friends, scout out the 'finers' (that's Kerry-speak for people you fancy), maybe even get your first kiss behind the shed after the *céilí* and generally just have the craic. Even though I was fluent in the language, I loved the chance to spend the summer

with my friends outside of school. And that year,
I was heading to the Gaeltacht 'on my own'. I was
absolutely, 100 per cent ready to make my mark.

> *I was eager to start*
> **Bhíos ar bís le tosú**

But before all my fun could start, Mom, Grandad
and I had travelled back to his hometown of Baile
na nGall on our annual visit; this summer would be
different for me, but we would keep our family tra-
dition. Sitting outside Tigh T.P.'s, with a Guinness
before him and smoking his pipe, he would look out
across Smerwick Harbour. He seemed right as rain to
me, but it was to be the last time we spent together
and the final time he would see Baile na nGall.

> *Nostalgia for the past*
> **Cumha i ndiaidh an tseansaoil**

In Feothanach, a small townland in the Kerry
Gaeltacht in Corca Dhuibhne west of Mount Brandon,

one of my cousins, Áine, was working as a *bean an tí* (woman of the house) and so I was effectively living with family for the three weeks which made me feel extra safe and happy. Ours was the furthest house from the main community hall where Irish lessons and the *céilí* (dance) were held. The community hall was the focal point of all of our Gaeltacht adventures, a major touchstone of our experience there, for it was where we all congregated when we first arrived and where we said goodbye at the end of the three weeks. We walked to and from it every day, a journey of twenty-five minutes on foot. If it rained, we took the bus. As quick as the bus was, I loved trudging back and forth on the road, talking with my friends about absolutely everything of importance: who we reckoned was an *actual* finer, what get-up we planned to wear at the evening's *céilí* and how being a teenager was just so hard.

> *We're celebrating our new-found freedom*
> **Táimid ag ceiliúradh saoirse a bhfuil muid nua aici**

The Gaeltacht was a place for us to kick back and though our teachers and *cinnirí* (leaders) were looking after us, it was new to have some freedom from our families. The gossip would begin at the breakfast table and continued well into the day's sporting activities and classes. I tragically didn't manage to pull a kiss, but there were plenty of lads who took my fancy.

Mom was on holidays with her friends in Italy while I was sauntering around the Gaeltacht with mine. This was long before roaming charges were abolished in the European Union and so we both just had to presume that the other was having a great time. The Gaeltacht was a bubble far from any school routine, our morning classes didn't feel like lessons. We weren't regurgitating stories and poetry. We got a new spin on pop music and clever tips for remembering key grammar rules. It was casual, practical learning. Naturally, I was having the time of my life. And at the end of the three weeks we had formed what felt like an inseparable bond until the end of our days. We were in absolute bits when it was time to leave and I had several brand new friends crying profusely on my shoulder at the community hall, promising to write letters to me as soon as they got home.

But unknown to us, while we were enjoying our own summer holidays, Grandad's health was declining quickly. He was a man who would only tell you how bad he was feeling after the fact anyway and Mom calls it a defence mechanism he set up for himself long before I came on the scene. He never wanted us to fuss over him and his health and he wanted to maintain his independence as much as possible even into old age.

> Death is the enemy of youth
> and the friend of old age
> **Is namhaid an bás don óige**
> **agus cara don sean**

Because I was young, perhaps I didn't realise how his movements and mind were failing. I always thought of him as a capable and self-sufficient man whose mind was as clear as day, always ready to play with me when I asked him to. But my cousin David tells a story from my grandad's later years when he forgot to choose self-raising flour for his famous *curney* bread – our own family recipe – and how he became so frustrated he spent the rest of the day giving out to himself saying things like, 'Well, that's it now'. David being older than me would have noticed little lapses like this. My grandfather's enormous pride meant losing the ability to do and remember small things was an attack on his very dignity.

Soon after I returned from the Gaeltacht, Mom got a call from her sister to come back from Italy. Grandad was packing his suitcase for Killarney Community

Hospital. He had bypassed his own doctor's care and was seeking more specialised treatment. He was taking things seriously, as he was finding it more and more difficult to even carry milk home from the shop next door, mere steps away. The doctors in Killarney told him he was going into heart failure. At fifteen years of age, I went into denial. The man who had been 'fine' a month ago, independent and his mind still clear, was dying? It seemed unlikely to me but my gut was telling me otherwise. We went to the hospital every day of the next two weeks. The time dragged but it was precious too, more important than any day of my childhood spent with him. I sat on the side of his bed and placed my hand on his, still warm and still strong. He had hardworking hands that had served him sodding the turf, gripping the handlebars of that black bicycle, holding mine as we walked to school. An overwhelming emotion pushed against my chest and I was fit to burst. I told him I loved him and I was glad he had been part of my life. As much as I wanted to, I didn't beg him to stay. A little later, Mom and I left the hospital to go get a sandwich in the small deli across the road and while we were ordering, my Mom's sister called to say he had slipped away. My whole body tensed up, and as I looked at my Mom, I couldn't believe the look on her face. I'd never seen anyone so sad before. She immediately took off back to the hospital but all I could do was amble back from the shop, crossing the road in slow motion. I can remember so clearly those deliberate steps that I took to get to his room. I was in a daze trying to process it but the more my brain tried to, the more it was like thinking through a blur. I sat in the corridor outside his room with my ham sandwich on my lap, staring at it silently. There was a clock overhead and every tick sounded like a gong. Eventually Mom ushered me in and even then, seeing his body just lying there with no rise in his chest, I couldn't comprehend what was going on – I refused to.

Thirteen years later, my cousin David and I truly believe he waited until we had left his side to let go, a final act of compassion so we wouldn't be even more torn apart. I know it must have taken him an incredible amount of energy and courage to admit it was his time. In hindsight, this is true to the person he was. He didn't want us to see him like that and I am hugely grateful to him that he waited for us to leave.

> *Death gives taste to life*
> **Bheireann an bás blas
> don bheatha**

The days between his wake and funeral were a mix of blurred and lucid moments. Though there were seventy-six years between us, he was like a father to me and I never thought I would be without him so early on in my life. Grandad was the only man in our house, just like the fathers of any of my friends. Sure, he didn't have the same energy to go out and play GAA with me every day, but I had always preferred to play with my Thomas the Tank Engine in the grass while chatting with him *as Gaeilge* anyway. With Grandad gone, we both felt we had lost a massive part of ourselves. Mom says she was relieved he didn't suffer a long and painful death, he got to simply pass away quietly and quickly. He had had a full life and though there was now a hole in hers, it was selfish for her to want to hold onto him. For her, it was important to let him go.

> *He was a man of dignity*
> **B'fhear uasal é**

We brought Grandad home to Tralee to wake him. I sat with him for most of that time in a daze until a moment when I looked out the window and saw a familiar face sitting on our wall: Johnín Phil O'Sullivan. I called out to Mom in the kitchen, and she went out to tell him of Grandad's passing, and that he was at home if he wanted to pay his respects. Moments later, I moved aside as Johnín placed one hand on the side of the coffin while his *caipín* was balled in the other hand. He looked at my Grandad with a stillness that made my eyes fill with tears.

After Johnín's gentle visit everything seemed to pick up pace when I wished that it would slow down. That evening songs were sung, stories were told, and our many neighbours and some local people paid their respects to a legend now gone forever. It was like a conveyor belt of people coming in and out of the house. In this *fuadar* (fuss) and as the hours went by, I knew I was coming closer to never seeing my him again and it broke my heart.

> *In loving memory of the departed*
> **I ndílchuimhne na marbh**

His funeral was one of the largest Tralee had ever seen. It felt something close to a state funeral. Family abroad flew home to attend and the few remaining people from his turf-cutting and Garda Síochána days were there. I could see my Gaelscoil teachers, people from Raidió na Gaeltachta, who had spoken to him on air many a time, and Grandad's family from 'back west'. The church was packed to the brim and it was comforting to see so many people. Respect was shown from the English- and Irish-speaking communities. Many of them I had never met before but they still held my hand in theirs and told me things about my Grandad I already knew to be true, that he was a kind and wonderful man who touched and enriched the lives of all who ever met him.

At the funeral, when the time came, I could barely choke out a Prayer of the Faithful. But true to form, Paddy Kavanagh had written his own appreciation to be read out at his funeral. No way would he have trusted us to write a decent one in our state, *ambaiste*. And though my heart was completely broken that day, I couldn't help but laugh at how even in death he was his own man and true to himself. My cousin David was the one who read it to the congregation of mourners. No one else had a copy of it in the church and hearing his words as they were read out brought the tears to my eyes, and still do. I have the appreciation still to this day pinned up on my notice board in my home.

An Garda Síochána gave him a full guard of honour outside the church with his *caipín* and the Irish flag sitting on top of his coffin. I can't tell you what the weather was like that day because it didn't matter to me. In my memory of the event, I stand in front of his grave, in the family plot with his wife, Winnie, and his two sons Paudie and Dan, and I bid him a *Slán go fóill*.

Almost immediately, our lives changed. Mom had already decided to retire that year, but now she had to find a new routine at home in Tralee, one without her father. The impact of his death would not hit her until much later and when it did, her sadness came in waves. The thought of Christmas at home that year horrified us, we couldn't imagine celebrating it 'alone' and so we began plans to go abroad.

Now, as an adult, I see Grandad's death as the moment I knew that I would use Irish in my day-to-day life, in my studies and in my work. In the years that followed – my Leaving Cert years – Irish became the only subject I cared about and I was adamant I was getting an A1. To me, the language was the last bit of living memory I had of my beloved grandfather and I was determined to cherish it. It was our connection to each other and to the people of the Gaeltacht who meant the world to us both.

# The Big Smoke

It was no surprise to me or anyone around me that Irish remained an integral part of my education, even after grandad passed away. The language was alive in me for the first fifteen years of my life and I just knew that I wanted that to continue into my career somehow. As a teenager, I was obsessed with the media, especially radio, and just like my grandad, I was an eager listener. The radio was a focal point in his home; even when Kerry matches were being broadcast on the television, he would only listen to the commentary on Raidió na Gaeltachta. My mom is also an avid radio listener tuning into RTÉ Radio One during the day and RTÉ Lyric FM in the evening.

Radio is something that we both enjoy, and we're not alone; recent JNLR figures show that Irish people are still dedicated listeners of radio. In late 2018, more than 3.17 million listeners over the age of fifteen tuned into radio every weekday, with 83% of all adults doing so daily for about four hours. And while some people listen to music-only shows, we listened to talk radio. It's like having another person in the room keeping you company and I love the fact that I don't have to stay in one place to experience it. On the school runs in the car with mom in the morning, I indulged in Today FM's 'Gift Grub', something to perk me up before I dragged myself into class, and at night I listened to talk radio just before I went to bed. I never had a television in my room but I always had a radio. I would turn the volume down just low enough that I could make out the voices of Ray Foley and J.P. Gilbourne on 'The Blast' as I drifted off to sleep.

> *I prefer radio to television*
> **Is fearr liom an raidió ná
> an teilifís**

Before we filled out our college applications, a conversation with the school's career guidance counsellor was standard procedure. But heading into his office, my future career was already obvious to me: I wanted to work in media and I specifically wanted Irish to be part of that too. The career counsellor told me media was far too precarious a career and that I'd be better off doing something dependable like medicine. I enjoyed pointing out to him that my lack of science subjects was likely to make a career in medicine precarious too! I was studying art, music, French and geography; not subjects that were going to make me 'Ireland's next best neurosurgeon'.

I was determined to do something involving *Gaeilge*, not just for myself but also to keep my memory of Grandad alive. He died the same summer as my Junior Certificate exams so he never saw that 'A' I wangled out of my Irish exam nor the 'A1' I got in my Leaving Certificate, but I'd like to think he knows somehow.

Even though my classmates and career counsellors considered English as the language of opportunity, at home I was always encouraged to use Irish to further my career. For my mother, it was Irish that was the language of opportunity and she would constantly remind me of how places like TG4, Raidió na Gaeltachta and RTÉ could do with an injection of diversity. She believed I'd be the woman to do that! Growing up, there was never anyone on our airwaves or screens that I could relate to as a person of colour (especially in the group of Irish-language presenters). There was simply no one that looked like me. But with my mom's encouragement I too began to believe that I could be a part of that change. I could be that person that I had longed so much to look up to.

In 2009, there were just four third-level institutions doing media and Irish-language courses, all of which I was interested in: University of Limerick, NUI

Galway, Dublin Institute of Technology and Dublin City University (DCU). Coming from Tralee, most of my friends were heading to University College Cork, but I chose DCU for its strong media course (alumni include broadcaster Matt Cooper, presenter Laura Whitmore, director Dearbhla Walsh and Noel Curran, former Director General of RTÉ). DCU was, and still is, a breeding ground for some of Ireland's most effective communicators. And, believe it or not, I was actually happy to move away from Kerry. As a family, we had often visited Dublin to see my godmother, Maria, and I felt like I knew the city better than Cork. Also, Dublin had a buzz about it that excited me. It seemed more diverse, not just in opportunity but in demographics too.

Moving to Dublin (or 'The Big Schmoke' as it's still known to us culchies) was a big deal. Despite growing up a 'townie', mom and I moved outside Tralee in 2000. We grew our own food and I became a bit of a farmer. It's then that I transformed into a 'culchie', wearing wellies to the compost heap and spending time brandishing a strimmer and rooting up weeds. I found myself very happy in the silence that country life offered and the close relationships with our neighbours and their relatives.

So, while I was excited for what Dublin would offer me, it was a massive leap to set off on a journey in the opposite direction to many of my peers. More importantly, for the first time ever, I had to plan my wardrobe! Packing for Dublin, I was swapping my wellies for boots and acquiring Penney's finest. It was like prepping for 'Paisean Faisean'. I switched from tracksuits to more jeans, shirts to polo necks and there was an influx of dresses into my suitcase. Like many first years, I was more nervous about how I looked than the actual move to Dublin.

> How's life in the big smoke?
> **Cad é mar atá an saol sa chathair mhór?**

So with several suitcases packed to the brim – the ones you save for with every tenner you spend in SuperValu – and the Volkswagen Golf loaded up, Mom and I headed to Dublin. Among my precious cargo was my grandad's copy of Dinneen's *Irish-English Dictionary*, a practical talisman of nostalgic importance to me. Dinneen's dictionary is one of the great lexicographical works published in Irish. It was compiled by An tAthair Pádraig Ó Duinnín (Reverend Patrick S. Dinneen) in 1904. Nothing of this scale had ever been put together before and the words that he used were rich in content. In the early 1900s, it was considered a modern reference tool of great significance. The original stock and plates of the dictionary were sadly destroyed during the Easter Rising in 1916, so Dinneen took that opportunity to expand the dictionary. He turned it into a beast of a book, 1,340 pages to be precise, which he compiled with the assistance of Liam S. Gogan and published in 1927.

It was like Paddy Kavanagh's second bible and the fact that Dinneen was also a Kerryman added brownie points for my grandad. Though he had a few editions himself, the one I inherited is a green hardback from 1965, a whole 1,344 pages long! This is the one I carried all the way to Dublin. For Irish-language speakers like my grandad, it was more than just a dictionary. Containing the most complete grammatical treatments of words, in-depth details of their usage as well as pronunciations, technical terms, idioms and poetic expressions, Dinneen's Irish-English dictionary was a document of the living speech of the people.

> *A good dictionary is your only man*
> **Foclóir maith, sin é a theastaíonn**

When we arrived in DCU, we hauled everything up the stairs to the student residence, my new home for the next year. Over the next hour, with small breaks, we moved everything into the apartment I would share with four other first years. When all was unpacked, and the car boot finally empty and closed, Mom had tears in her eyes as she bid me *slán*. But I wasn't sad, I was on an adventure! This is it, I thought, I'm on my own, fending for myself!

I arrived a week before my course began and quickly discovered it was going to take a lot of energy to make new friends. I didn't know anyone from my hometown and so introducing myself felt really awkward. Anytime I met someone new at Fresher events I felt like I was speed dating.

'Hey, how are you?'

'What course are you doing?'

'Do you know anyone here?'

'What do you like to do?'

My head was in a whirl with all the questions. I had to mentally prepare myself anytime I was venturing out of my apartment and, once there, I would stand awkwardly near the exit so I could escape if I needed to. At home in Tralee I was able to keep to myself and no one bothered me much. But here, in DCU, in Dublin, in my new life, there were so many people who wanted to say 'hello'. It was mind-boggling and

I hadn't expected to feel this way at all. How on earth was I going to survive?

> *There was a nervous quiver in her voice*
> **Bhí creathán neirbhíseach ina guth**

And living with strangers; that was going to be interesting. I had met one, Chris from Wicklow, when I had arrived with my suitcases, and he seemed sound enough. I wondered was he feeling as anxious as I was and what he was like at home. Was he, like me, trying to appear confident? The apartment had only the basic things, an oven, table, chairs, couch and vacuum cleaner, but despite it being a relatively empty space the whole situation overwhelmed me and I found myself overthinking everything. Do we rotate turns when we want to use the Henry Hoover? What is the etiquette when we run out of Lee Strand milk? DO THEY EVEN HAVE LEE STRAND?! When would it be socially acceptable to tell them I needed to go for a nap, and would they mind keeping it down? Christ, I had never had to live with anyone not related to me before and I felt out of my depth. In secondary school I didn't consider myself 'one of the girls' and was more interested in video games, alternative music, and keeping to myself and had mastered the means of blending in. In college, there was nowhere to hide, and I could've done with a 'how to be a normal student' manual.

> *She felt overwhelmed by everything*
> **Mhothaigh sí go raibh gach rud ag dul sa mhuileann uirthi**

Along with Chris, I lived with Will (also from Wicklow), and two girls, Dearbhail from Laois and Heather from Tipperary. We were able to bond over not being city kids and we often talked about how different things were in Dublin. The colour of my skin or where I was 'really from' was never brought up. I was relieved, they knew what it was like to come from the countryside! Hurray, we can talk! In the end, all of my anxiety was for nought as they were the soundest people and we got on like a house on fire.

> *We lived on toast*
> **Bhíomar beo ar thósta**

I'm an ambivert at heart and I get panic attacks, so when entering new social situations, it's easier for me to dip in or observe from afar, and then zip out the door in an 'Irish Goodbye'. There was a lot of 'Noooope' when it came to group interactions and it could be mighty stressful. I had to take regular breaks in my room between socialising and being with new people. It would be a few interactions before I could warm up to new people because it took a hell of a lot of energy for me to prepare myself to even just say 'hello'.

What I did notice, though, even in my brief interactions with the Freshers of my year, is that they were a global bunch. DCU had many international students, particularly from Asia and, initially, seeing them mingle made my heart soar. It was the first time I was in an educational environment with people of Asian heritage. But that feeling subsided quickly. In truth, I didn't feel like I could totally relate to them because I wasn't an international student myself and I couldn't speak any languages from Asia either. I was Irish, just with a different skin colour. There was only one place where I felt like I would make immediate friends and that was on my course, Irish and media.

My degree, a Bachelor of Arts in Gaeilge agus Iriseoireacht (Irish and Journalism), was new and we were set to be only the third wave of graduates. With a

BIC four-colour pen in my hand and a notepad in the other (as well as, for some reason, a shatterproof ruler!), I waltzed into the Fiontar labs (our faculty rooms), ready to indulge my nerdy self. I had made it through my orientation week without any major hurdles so I knew that I could do it. After all, the students on my course all loved Irish as much as I did.

With only nine others on my course, there was no avoiding getting to know my peers. Immediately, I gravitated towards three of them, Fran, Liam and Jill. I had briefly met Jill during orientation week, a Clarewoman from Feakle, close to where my grandmother was born. She has a sense of style that I love – vintage with the best dress hauls from charity shops. Jill is classy. What I admired most about Fran was her ambition. She always made it clear that she wanted to work at the BBC or as an editor at an influential media corporation far from her home in Kildare. She was no slacker and I loved that about her. I wanted to be as good as she was, and I worked hard to match her ambition.

With so few of us on my course, we joined the business students for many of our modules, like *teangeolaíocht* (linguistics) and *feasacht teanga* (language awareness) and Liam from Wicklow was taking the Gaeilge and Gnó (Irish and Business) course. He also knew my roommates Will and Chris, and never failed to make me laugh. He was super sassy which I did, and still do adore about him. He introduced me to Lady Gaga and we learned the dances to 'Bad Romance' and 'Telephone' which we loved to break out at the club! It was a bond for life.

Most of my modules were delivered completely in Irish and I was 'delira and excira'. This complete immersion was just what I had wanted in choosing my university course. My secondary school had not been an all-Irish one and I had missed that full-time exposure I had had in primary school. We took a variety of subjects that included television, radio and writing as well as mandatory and necessary grammar lessons that got into the nitty-gritty of the language. I did my best to keep on top of it but it turned out I wasn't as nerdy as I had thought I was. Some of my classmates, particularly Fran who picked up Irish grammar like a pro, were just as obsessed as I was about Irish, and I made lifelong friends. I am forever grateful to these friends for helping me realise that Lee Strand milk is a Kerry-only brand …

---

*Friendship is a two-way street*
**Oibríonn an cairdeas an dá bhealach**

---

We, the Gaeilge agus Iriseoireacht (also known as GIs) and the Gaeilge agus Gnó (the GGs), were a close group and many of our adventures were fuelled by our love for the Irish language. What I also loved was that I was immediately accepted for me and I never had to explain my adoption or my skin colour to any of them even though I was clearly the only person on my course with Asian heritage. This meant a lot to me. Before arriving on campus, I had prepared the spiel about my background, but it never once came up and I respected them for that. Most of the students came from outside of Dublin and even though none of them were from Kerry I still felt a mutual understanding between us as we tried to make it in The Big Smoke.

We especially did ourselves proud in our one and only escapade to the Oireachtas. Not to be confused with the Houses of the Oireachtas (which for a bunch of first years would be minus craic; shout out to Fran for that phrase!), Oireachtas na Gaeilge is an annual festival of Irish arts and culture, which began in 1897. Divided into two events, the visual arts element is held in April and May and the big celebration comes at the end of October or the start of November. The very first Oireachtas was organised by Conradh na Gaeilge (The Gaelic League), as part of a wider move-ment to rediscover Gaelic heritage. These days, more than 8,000 people attend the annual event. Since the

1970s, Oireachtas has been held in different towns and cities across Ireland – the one my friends and I went to was in my home county of Kerry.

> *It was absolute madness!*
> **Ní raibh ann ach mire ó**
> **thús deireadh!**

The Oireachtas is like an Irish-language version of Electric Picnic. With competitions like Comórtas na mBan (sean-nós singing competition for women), Comórtas na bhFear (for men), Corn Uí Riada (for all ages) and the Comórtas Damhsa ar an Sean Nós 'steip' (free-style dancing competition), if you've even an inkling of interest in Irish culture then it's a must. Normally I wouldn't have had much interest in the dancing, but as the band picked up their instruments, I found myself dancing with my friends to all the jigs and reels. What got me most, however, was that it brought everyone together regardless of their level of Irish or their age. I was astounded at this equality as I hadn't expected it outside of my Gaeltacht bubble 'back west'. While my friends and I were chugging Fat

Frogs and Captain Morgan, I was aware of what an amazing *seisiún* (session) it was.

> *The mother and father*
> *of all hangovers*
> **Póit an diabhail**

While I might not remember *every*thing about Oireachtas, thanks to my good friend, Jameson, I do remember the thrill of being with my friends celebrating something innate to us: the Irish language. It felt totally empowering to be able to blend in with thousands of people and use Irish so naturally outside of my home and outside of our college bubble. I was out in the open, amongst a massive crowd of people and I wasn't even in the Gaeltacht! I spoke a language that everyone there loved, therefore nothing else mattered. I was accepted.

> *That was some craic*
> **A leithéid de chraic**

While there was a healthy dose of fun and frolics, and I was finding my way in the world, my degree pushed me to seriously consider my options in expanding my skillset. If I was going to make it in the media world, I'd have to do more than just turn up for lectures and conquer Irish grammar. But when you're an eighteen-year-old and fresh out of secondary school, these developments don't seem that obvious or urgent. My friend Alanna would talk about all the extra things that she was doing outside of lecturers. When she made the point that a degree doesn't automatically get you a job, it was a 'duh' moment for me and I duly took note. With my heart still set on being a future presenter of 'Morning Ireland', my friends and I signed up to join the volunteer team of our college radio station. I made a weekly Irish-language current affairs show, called 'Freagraí na Seachtaine' with two friends from my course and, thankfully, there's not a trace of it online anywhere so no one will ever hear just how *amateur* amateur radio can be. Apart from learning that 'don't push that button' really means don't push that button, we also learned valuable lessons on teamwork and coming up with things on the fly, and discovered how difficult it often is to find people who will speak Irish in interviews.

Ever since I created extra-curricular activities for myself, I've been the kind of person who has hands in various pots and in college it was like I owned a small ceramics factory! By day I was attending lectures and in my spare time I was co-editing the Irish-language section of the university's newspaper, *The College View*, presenting radio shows and running the website of Cumann Gaelach (DCU's Irish language society). My summers in college were spent working as an *ard-chinnire* (senior leader) on Irish-language courses in Dundalk and Drumree at Coláiste na bhFiann. There, I felt like a 'proper' adult ready to take on the world even though I wasn't even twenty. My students actually listened to me even though some of us were close in age and many were significantly taller than me (I'm only five foot one!). I felt respected and it was the greatest feeling.

During my final year at DCU I took the reins as Irish editor of *The College View*. My friend Fran had been my editor the previous year. Things were going well, I felt like I had really made my mark at DCU, and the university experience helped me realise that I enjoyed being busy and that I had tonnes of ambition to succeed.

> There is no fat without labour
> **Ní fhaightear saill gan saothar**

Even though I was exposed to lots of Irish in college, I just couldn't get enough of it. In my first year, in 2009, I approached Raidió RíRá, an Irish-language, Dublin-based radio station still in its infancy and run by volunteers. It was a real no-brainer for them: I was an Irish media student and they needed volunteers, so I was accepted right away. I co-hosted a music show (but for the life of me I can't remember the name of it!) from their small studio in the city centre and dabbled in horrific Photoshop creations like banners for the website designed to entice people to click in.

My college years (2009–12), coincided with the rise of social media and I became an early adopter of it. It all began when our technology lecturer told us there was this website called 'Twitter' where people wrote witty commentary, news organisations shared their stories and they could all only use 140 characters to get their point across. This conciseness intrigued me. I was used to writing melancholic online diary entries and lengthy paragraphs on Xanga.com (cringe!) but this Twitter thing sounded different. I hopped on, signed up with @unakavanagh as my Twitter handle and started tweeting to my heart's content. I immediately fell head over heels in love with it. I had access to people all over the world, including the journalists I admired, and I had global and immediate access to news.

Twitter was a positive thing for me. It gave me an outlet to express myself and start building an influencing profile outside of the world of college. It was on Twitter that I was approached in 2010 by former RTÉ journalist Mark Little to intern at his news aggregation site, Storyful. (He later sold it for €18million!) As I built up my profile, it became clear to me that I was making some sort of a mark. People liked my commentary about Irishness, identity and racism. They also liked my jokes. Win-win!

I had a MacBook Pro for college work and with its slick video and audio editing software at my fingertips, I was immediately encouraged to create. YouTube and Twitter were my 'babies' and I became a self-taught video editor and content creator both in English and *as Gaeilge*. By expanding my platforms, I was able to share more of the person behind the tweets so people could see me 'in real life'. YouTube was still in its infancy then, but the pleasure that I got from a whole day working on a video was worth the handful of views it would attract.

My lectures on journalism ethics, presentation and Irish grammar as well as my evenings spent editing, organising files and upskilling were a million miles away from the welly-wearing Úna-Minh, picking tomatoes and courgettes in my quiet Tralee home. But by homing in on what I loved doing – being part of the vibrant and fresh online world – I was excited and energised by this completely new world and immediate access to information.

It's true, though, that in my first years in Dublin, I was always close to burnout. But I was young (even younger than I am now!), curious and I loved being so busy. In secondary school I had juggled stage school, piano lessons, rowing, grinds and art classes. Maybe it was a fear of missing out but it made no difference to me to be busy in college too. I guess it allowed me to forget the way the world might see me and concentrate on things that brought me joy. Now, I think I was looking for what I considered a 'normal' existence with people my age and where my skin colour or heritage weren't the first topics of conversation. I really did just adore the Irish language and, in time, I found I had moved on from my original reason for coming to Dublin. I think I needed the time away from Tralee to really appreciate the gift that my grandad had given me. As a young adult, finding myself and my way in the Big Smoke, I wasn't just doing it for the memory of him, I was finally doing it for myself.

# 'Where Are You Really From?'

I've had more than my fair share of racism and general ignorance in my life. From the casual racism by a taxi driver or shop assistant to being jeered at and shoved in the street, it's all game for some people. Apart from it being obviously problematic and nasty, the underlying effect of having to deal with the same insults and questions again and again is extremely frustrating because I've grown up all my life knowing I'm Irish – not Irish-Vietnamese, not Vietnamese – simply Irish.

> *You shouldn't judge by appearances*
> **Ní hionann i gcónaí an cófra is a lucht**

Meeting new people can be … interesting. I smile and I'm polite and I feel like they're just waiting for me to say something they consider 'non-Irish' so they can interrupt with, 'AH HA! So, you're clearly not *really* one of us'. Their desire to 'catch me out' has made me wary of strangers and new situations. Since my early college days, I've learned how to prepare myself for new surroundings and people. But that in turn burns a lot of my own energy so then it's even more exhausting having to prove something as inherent and undeniable as my Irish identity. Only in Ireland – my home! – am I a curiosity, no matter how many times I've spoken publicly about my identity.

Taxis are very often the scenes of this nonsense, passed off as casual banter. As a result, I try to avoid them now. After hopping in and confirming that, yes, indeed I am the person they were meant to pick up, the conversation starts with that most innocent of questions:

'Oh, where are you from?'

'Oh I'm from Kerry,' I respond, knowing exactly what is coming next. As the conversation moves on, the driver becomes more probing and less polite. They glance between my reflection in their rear-view mirror and my name on the taxi app.

'Úna-Minh Kavanagh … Yeah, but where are you really from?'

'I'm from Kerry but I'm a freelancer so I work around the country.'

'Yes, but, where are your people from?'

'My people? Well my Mom is also from Kerry and a lot of my family are from the Gaeltacht.'

'And was learning another language easy since, you know …?'

'No I love Irish, it's great, my grandad spoke to me in Irish all the time.'

And on and on and on.

I'm no fool, I know that what they're really asking is: why are you brown? It's not that people of colour are hypersensitive to or offended by being asked 'where are you from?' It's the lack of acceptance dressed up as incredulity that is ridiculous and rude. We're just so tired of having to explain ourselves and our heritage all the time, especially because people don't take our first answer – where we *are* from – as the truth. Would I lie to you? My partner, who is a white Irishman is never probed about where he is *really* from when we're in Ireland. My mom is never asked, nor was my grandad asked either. I lived in Dublin for ten years of my adulthood, a city where people from all across the world have made their home, and yet I was regularly on the receiving end of the belief that being white automatically means you're Irish. This discrimination grinds a person down and I'm not unique in feeling this. Indeed, the director of the European Network Against Racism (ENAR) Ireland, Shane O'Curry, put it well when he described how the 'drip, drip, drip effect' of casual racism turns 'corrosive' and wears on the person. Oh, I can relate.

> *I'm only human*
> **Níl ionam ach duine tar éis
> an tsaoil**

By the time I started working as a journalist in Dublin at the age of twenty-one, after completing my degree in 2012, I had become used to hearing racial slurs thrown at me. I was working on Capel Street where I could frequent a Brazilian shop, an Italian café, a Korean Barbecue, a Japanese restaurant and even a Vietnamese café called Aobaba. The street felt safe and I was spoiled for choice when it came to seeking lunch options. No one looked at me twice. I went to Aobaba frequently to savour its Vietnamese menu, food which was familiar to me after some recent trips to Vietnam. But when I left that street for the rest of the city, I needed to avoid hassle and I did that by putting on my headphones, dipping my head down and walking on. I could be doing anything or nothing – walking down Henry Street, hanging out in St Stephen's Green or getting a takeaway with my mates – and some dope would yell at me something stupid like 'What's the craic Miss Ping Pong?'

A year later, I had had enough of the slurs, all I wanted to do was go about my daily business, not feeling on the defence all the time. And so there I was, on a rare, sunny Thursday in May, standing on Parnell Street minding my own business, after another day at work and looking at my phone. I had spotted the group of young people, about ten or so teenagers, coming towards me from across the street and had consciously dipped my gaze to the screen, my default diversion tactic. When I looked up, it was just in time to hear one of the boys shout at me:

'You're a fucking chink.'

Once again I found myself bored and irritated having to defend myself. It was a sunny day in early summer, I was paying them no attention, why couldn't they just leave me alone? I reacted quickly, without thinking, without politeness, exhaling an exasperated, 'Oh, fuck off!' But as I spoke, the one who had shouted at me grabbed my face with his right hand and yanked at it. I stumbled out of shock and the force of it. Then he spat in my face.

Utter humiliation.

The gang moved on, all laughing and giving each other playful arm jabs. They left me to wipe the spit off my face and hair. I stood alone, phone in hand, my stomach churning with shame, fright and anger.

No one came to my aid.

My grandad, Paddy Kavanagh, was tall and handsome and rode his bicycle everywhere. He called it the 'poor man's Mercedes'.

Granny Winnie with her *madra* Wewak, named after the town in Papua New Guinea where Mom worked as an overseas volunteer in the early 1970s.

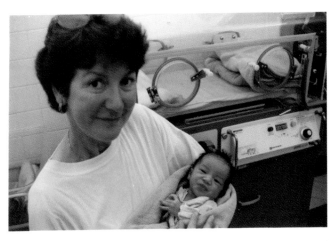

Meeting my mom, Noreen, for the first time in Bach Mai Hospital, Hanoi, in July 1991. I had a fine head of hair on me!

Mom signing my adoption papers in Bach Mai Hospital. Nguyet, her interpreter, is by her side.

Grandad was a hands-on father figure to me. He was seventy-five years old when I arrived, retired ten years, and a whole new chapter of his life was about to begin.

I was never without my milk bottle as a child, even while travelling on the back of my mom's bike. Here I am back west in the Kerry Gaeltacht, the Sleeping Giant in the background.

It was essential that we head back to the Gaeltacht every summer. This photograph was taken at the pier at Baile na nGall, our home away from home.

Learning the important life lesson of eye contact with former Tánaiste, Dick Spring, at an event in a bookshop in Tralee.

Grandad always donned his *caipín* when we were off on our adventures. I still have the one in this photograph.

'Úna-Minh, anseo!' Can you tell I was excited for my first day at school?

My grandad remained a dapper dresser into his later years. And he passed on his love of cycling to me. Together on our bikes we were dynamite!

Me, myself and John Deere. I am oozing the determination of any Kerry farmer.

"Tá péire slipéar faighte agamsa," arsa Tomás.
"Tá péire agamsa freisin," arsa Eithne.

Grandad loved 'correcting' the Irish in my storybooks to *fíor-Ghaelainn Chiarraí* (real Kerry-Irish). In his beautiful handwriting he wrote in the *seanchló* (old font).

This is the last photo taken of Paddy Kavanagh, just a few weeks before he died in the summer of 2006. He sits outside Tigh T.P.'s in his hometown of Baile na nGall, content with his pipe and pint.

Mom was incredibly proud when I graduated from Dublin City University in 2012 with a degree in Gaeilge agus Iriseoireacht (Irish and Journalism).

Video games have always played a massive part in my life, from *Pokémon* in primary school to live-streaming *Fallout: New Vegas* on Twitch *as Gaeilge*. Turning my passion into my occupation has made me a modern 'everyday Gaeilgeoir'.

While I was researching the #WeAreIrish project, I drew and tweeted this sketch as a response to the racism I experience again and again. These are real things that have been said to me over the years but they all enhance my armour. I am stronger than any of these words.

We share our Irishness and pride regardless of the colour of our skin. I am so grateful that so many people chose to be a part of #WeAreIrish, my first social media diversity campaign.

On one of the busiest streets in our capital city, not a single person nearby asked if I was okay. An older white man, sitting in a taxi about a metre from me, looked away when my eyes met his. All of those people around me saw exactly what had gone down but they walked on. I guess you could call this a prime example of the 'bystander effect', where multiple people see an incident and think someone should get involved but everyone waits for someone else to do something first and, in the end, no one does anything. I was absolutely furious to experience this first-hand. If you're wondering what they could have done differently, I can tell you that simply asking, 'Are you okay?' or 'Is there anything I can do?' goes a long way in the aftermath of such an attack. I needed empathy in that moment but the strangers around me made me feel like I didn't matter.

I had never gone to the Gardaí before about any racist incidents, because I always thought I'd be wasting their time. Ireland has the highest rates of some hate crimes in the EU, but no proper hate crime laws to address it, a statistic I was aware of for years and had, like many others, simply accepted. *Why bother?* I'd often think. These kinds of crimes were not in the news or on social media then like they are now; over the years I had learned to absorb racism silently and alone. I tended not to share most of these racist incidents with my mom because I didn't want to upset her even though I knew she would be in my corner. I didn't want her worrying about me. But on this day I walked home to my apartment in Stoneybatter, my mind on overdrive with a new purpose. As I reached the bottom of the stairs in my building, I gripped the bannister and took a breath. I was sick of dealing with this on my own. There and then the whole notion of 'céad míle fáilte' and the apparent friendliness our country prides itself on became a gross lie to me. I thought that if I, an Irishwoman and a person of colour, was getting this crap, what on earth were the immigrants to this country and our tourists receiving? I needed to do something about it.

I called the Gardaí at Store Street Garda Station a few hours after the attack and managed to get the words out. Even though my grandad had been a Garda, I had never had any dealings with them myself so I was a bit fearful going into an unknown situation. One of the first questions the Gardaí asked after taking my initial statement was:

'Why did you wait until now to report it?'

I'm sure it was just a standard question, but it threw me off. I felt like they were almost saying to me, 'Well clearly it wasn't too bad if you left it for a while before you rang us up.' But if I'm being honest, I also felt kind of silly approaching an authority like the Gardaí when they could be dealing with something I considered to be much more serious. I felt shame and guilt. A group of young, ignorant boys racially abused me and one of them spat at me. I was the adult in the situation. I was still standing and wasn't physically hurt. I began to question whether it was a real crime at all. But sometime after making my statement to the guards, and the more I thought about it, the more I realised I should not have felt silly or embarrassed to report this aggression towards me. Keeping quiet about it, *literally* keeping my head down and not reacting, would allow it to keep happening to me and to others just like me. I thought of the man in the taxi who wouldn't meet my pleading eyes and how this inaction confirmed my worst fears: people just don't believe it happens. Or, worse, they wilfully choose to ignore it even when it's right in front of them.

> *We have the right to speak out*
> **Tá sé de cheart againn**
> **labhairt amach**

So, having made my report to the guards, there was no way I was just going to sit around waiting for justice. Me being me, I posted my anger about the whole thing on Twitter and within minutes the reaction was loud and clear: horror mingled with an immense show of support. I just wish I could have had that response when I was standing there on the street on my own. Don't get me wrong, I value my online life, but there is still something better and more comforting about someone asking if you need help in real life. After that attack, I could've done with a hug and a cup of tea, not just a tweet.

In the weeks following the attack, using my own influence, I was able to push the story extensively, both online and off, to many media outlets. I was determined to show that I would not stand idly by simply taking it. I was on 'Ireland AM' and 'Midweek' on TV3 (now Virgin Media One); I wrote a piece for *The Irish Times* and *The Kerryman*; I was featured on The Journal.ie, Today FM, RTÉ Radio One, Newstalk and my own regional station, Radio Kerry. I also wrote a blog post that was viewed over 75,000 times. I was even interviewed for *The New York Times*. David Conrad, a PhD student, had spotted my story and wanted to write about what it meant to be Irish in Ireland today, as well as discrimination here. This unexpected international attention was a boon as it gave more gravitas to the story, one that could now be reaching Irish-Americans. All of this coverage and attention transformed an extremely negative and upsetting experience into a positive one.

The scale of it made me realise the strength of my own influence and reach, but also that I had a power I wanted to use responsibly. Despite some of my introvert tendencies, I was truly delighted to get my message through all that social media noise. This really was the moment when I took activism seriously. In a strange twist of fate, it was the catalyst I needed. My actions helped to raise awareness of racism in Ireland and, in turn, it forced open a conversation on the whole concept of Irishness. Because most people understood and agreed that what that boy did to me was wrong, what they hadn't thought about before was the fact that not every Irish person is white. That young thug had made the false deduction that what a person looks like is the equivalent of how that person identifies. Little did he know just how well connected I was and how much louder and stronger my voice could be.

**Derek Landy**
@DerekLandy
Everyone show their love for @unakavanagh, an Irish girl who was racially abused in Dublin. For taking a stand, Una ROCKS.

**Itayi Viriri**
@itayiviriri
Replying to @unakavanagh
@unakavanagh @IrishTimes ~ Well done for not taking this ignorant crap anymore! Too many of us do & that's wrong! Hopefully not any more!

**Laura**
@TheDublinDiary
Replying to @unakavanagh
@unakavanagh I read your blog post with my class of inner city learners yesterday, they were quite horrified, we talked at length about it.

**~ fionnuala ~**
@babyeatyrdingo
Replying to @unakavanagh
@unakavanagh @IrishTimes Too few people excuse racism as 'humour' in Ireland – thank you for speaking up and exposing the reality of it.

And finally, there was this comment on my original blogpost from my amazing mom:

**noreen kavanagh/una minh*s mum**
May 31, 2013
*Una Minh … you are a wonderful, brave, beautiful young woman … I am so proud of you. I feel so saddened, as your Mum, that you experience such awful racism … it says so much about the people doing it. I am so proud of you … you are bright and brave and courageous . . . It is not what happens to us in life Una Minh but how we handle it … that's what counts. You have my support and love all the way.*
*Momxx*

A minority, however, accused me of pulling the 'race card', eventually concluding, 'Ah sure, they were only messing'. One such absolute *amadán* decided to write to me anonymously:

> *Why do you claim to be Irish and European? You are Vietnamese. Some stupid paddy may have adopted you due to your own family and race throwing you into the bushes and not wanting you. But you are not one of us. Stop trying to steal our ethnicity and racial identity. If you want an identity go home and find it.*

I didn't bother responding to this *smugachán* (arse-hole). Waffle like this only reinforced my reasons for amplifying my story so firmly in the media in the first place. These racists can only consider being Irish as one thing: white, and if you don't fit into that description, you'll always be 'foreign' and therefore bad and 'other'. 'Playing the race card' is, in fact, a deeply harmful statement used to silence people of colour who dare to speak about their own, true experiences of racism. The race card just isn't a thing. Let me be very clear, I speak about racism because I've experienced it first-hand and the last thing I want to do is compete with anyone else on the aspects of it that matter most. A 'race card' suggests a kind of privilege or free pass yanked out by people of colour in order to win an argument. Things could not be further from the truth. Where the privilege actually lies is in not having to think about race issues, ever. This is not a game and I'm not trying to *win* anything. I'd actually really like to just blend in. In an equal world, the colour of my skin would never be brought up. But it is, constantly, by racists. Those who accuse me of using a 'race card' are attempting to shut down discussion (that racism exists is not up for debate, mind you). They're not interested in understanding my side of things, and thus they resort to this strange anger. People of colour keep being racially abused and many won't believe them until they're severely beaten up or killed. So frankly, one mere 'card' could never hold all the reasons why I would want to challenge racism.

Nearly a month had gone by when I was called in to the Garda Station to point out the gang of boys on CCTV. From this the Gardaí were able to identify the members of the group and begin questioning them (turns out that they, and particularly the boy who attacked me, were known to the Gardaí anyway). Four months later, I met with the boy who spat at me – let's call him 'John' – face-to-face for the first time since the attack. Because what happened to me was classified as an assault, I could have brought him to court, but I chose not to and instead opted for a different approach; I wanted to give him a chance for change. That meeting in October was part of a system called restorative justice (RJ), where the attacker meets with the victim to discuss the consequences of their actions and the way it has affected the people involved. John looked smaller than I remembered. After all this time, and all the talk about him, it was strange to see him there in front of me.

'I'm sorry', he mumbled, after being prompted by his social worker to start the conversation. Throughout this meeting, John was hunched over with his hands in his pockets. I reckoned he was about twelve years old. We were seated in a circle in a clinical room in a community centre in Stoneybatter, on chairs and tables stacked against the light blue walls. It was like a classroom set up for story time. There were eleven people in the room – his and my family, three Gardaí and a social worker. My mom had travelled up from Kerry to be there, and my partner, Pádhraic, joined us for support. The eleventh member of the group might have been in training but that's where my memory of that intense day begins to break down. I felt nauseous and light-headed; I could feel the tension. I felt like a guinea pig to RJ, unsure who it was designed to benefit, me the victim or John the perp. There were so many people with clipboards in the room that it looked like some sort of social experiment.

'Can you tell me about what happened?' the Garda facilitator asked us, papers resting on their lap.

Each one of us described our involvement in the assault, what had happened on the day and how we felt it had affected us and the other people involved. When I looked over at John I thought he looked bored. There were times when he yawned and looked at the ground and there were times when he shoved his hands into his pockets again and didn't engage – but I had been prepared for that behaviour. I'd known a few weeks before that I would have to meet him and I had mentally gone over various outcomes. But when he described what he had done to me, how he had spat at me and grabbed me, the horror of that moment on Parnell Street came flooding back to me. It was strange to see the words come out of his mouth and it was unsettling to hear his admission. I gripped the chair and silly thoughts came into my head, 'Why did I react?' or 'Why didn't I respond to him in Irish?' But just as quickly I scolded myself for dwelling on delayed emotions. I was becoming stronger.

I sensed little or no empathy in his voice, it was robotic, but when his parents spoke about how they felt when the Gardaí called to their home, they expressed sincere sadness and regret. Several years later, as I recall forty-five minutes of restorative justice, I'm tired all over again as I still try to figure out how the boy was feeling when he met me. But for me, it was about meeting my young aggressor and getting him to see I was just like him – another Irish person. It was important to me that he know his actions had hurt a person. So I told him I was saddened by his actions but I was also glad I had been able to turn his attack into an awareness campaign. I told him how the story had been covered by media in Ireland and in *The New York Times* and how many people were disappointed that a young man like him who could have a bright future could do such a thing and then laugh about it. My Mom told him of her heartbreak when I called her about his attack, and she told him she hoped he would learn from this and become a fine young man. But throughout the whole interaction, the boy made no eye-contact with any of us. Despite this, when it was all over, I looked him in the eye, extended my hand to his and shook it. For what it was worth, I wanted him to know that by choosing restorative justice instead of pressing charges, I had given him the opportunity to avoid time inside.

There is plenty of racism and xenophobia in Ireland, but it is covered strangely in the Irish media. Instead of giving a person of colour a platform to share their experience or talk about how to prevent or deal with racism, radio, television and print media invite the most controversial figures to write columns or talk on panels. I don't plan on giving them space in my book. But I will go so far as to say that I don't think we have yet developed the tools to proactively prevent racism from happening again. We are stuck in some kind of a PC reaction vortex. Then, when racism is reported – in the news, on social media, or in 'casual banter' in a WhatsApp group – we respond with naïve shock, total denial or those last lines of defence: 'Well, *I'm* not offended by it' or 'Stop being such a snowflake.'

> *The taint of racism*
> **Smál an chiníochais**

So, let us really consider what's going on with Irish identity today. And let's admit one truth right now: Irish people, no matter where they come from, are migrant people. The whole concept of identity has changed radically in recent years. Look it up in a dictionary and it is still defined as some deep-rooted and permanent concept, but in an ultra-connected and mobile world, identity can actually be quite fragile and we must allow it to change with the times.

> *We must accept that things change*
> **Caithfimid glacadh leis go n-athraíonn rudaí**

These days, around one in six Irish people live abroad and nearly the same percentage (17%) of those living in Ireland were not born here. Ireland has the highest percentage of its population living abroad of any developed country and around 180 different nationalities have come to live here. The number of people in Ireland holding dual nationality – Irish and another – has increased since the 2011 census by 87.4% to 104,784 persons (5.87% of the population). We are a multicultural society and I for one wish to celebrate that.

> *Modern Irish society is multi-ethnic*
> **Tá sochaí na hÉireann il-eitneach sa lá atá inniu ann**

For many, their language is part of their identity and speaking multiple languages is what makes us more diverse as a society. The 2016 census found that 612,000 Irish residents spoke a foreign language at home with Polish, French, Romanian and Lithuanian being the most commonly spoken languages other than English and Irish. But many of these speakers are also Irish-born. By contrast, only 73,000 spoke Irish daily outside of the educational system. The truth is that today an Irish person is two times more likely to use Polish as they are Irish. But nearly 1.76 million people (nearly 37% of the population) stated they could speak Irish. Of those who spoke Irish daily, 20.2% lived in Dublin City and its suburbs (incidentally, this was an increase on the 2011 Census). This is a positive thing. Cork, Galway and Limerick together accounted for 8.2% of daily Irish speakers and outside of these cities, the largest absolute numbers of daily speakers were living in An Bun Beag-Doirí Beaga (a townland in the Gaoth Dobhair Gaeltacht in Donegal), Letterkenny and Swords. Predictably, daily Irish speakers in the Gaeltacht areas of Galway and Donegal made up almost three quarters of speakers in Gaeltacht areas. Who knows what the 2021 census will show? One thing is for sure though: I see an appetite online for the Irish language I use there daily and I've never been left hanging when I seek conversations *as Gaeilge*. In addition, the interactions I see in learner's circles are overwhelmingly encouraging.

On Duolingo, the language-learning app and website that boasts 300 million members worldwide, they proudly declare that there are more users learning the Irish language than there are native Irish speakers. In Ireland, we have a unique opportunity to enhance our sense of Irish identity with a unique language. It's there for anyone who may want to learn it, regardless of how they identify or where they come from originally. Hence, there is more of a chance now than ever before for it to grow from a minority language back into a flourishing one. People want to learn Irish and I for one am optimistic.

> They gain a sense of their own identity
> **Faigheann siad tuiscint ar a bhféiniúlacht féin**

I have never understood the reasons for the racism I have experienced in Ireland. There will always be those who want to turn migration and globalisation into an 'us' vs 'them' conflict. We've all heard statements like, 'They're coming over here, taking our jobs' and 'We have a housing crisis, how can we bring even more of them in?!' But this makes no sense to me when I think of all the Irish emigrants who have been other nations' 'them' many a time. Our long history of emigration to America and Australia, as well as the arrival of Celts, Vikings, Christians and Normans means that we know what it's like to be on the move, putting down new roots and becoming citizens of another place. We know what it's like to have to abandon our language in favour of the common one or the coloniser's tongue and we know in our bones how devastating it is to be forced off our lands. For centuries, we have had to depend on the kindness of other nations. That we have migration and integration in our DNA means that I've always been baffled about the racism I experience and see in Ireland.

> *Culture is deeply enmeshed with the national identity*
> **Tá dlúthcheangal idir an cultúr agus an fhéiniúlacht náisiúnta**

And look, I get why people are curious about me. I'm not an eejit, I know I was born in Vietnam (there was never a time when I didn't know this, such was the openness of my mother and my grandfather), but these days being Irish is more than just where you were born. I've an Irish accent – which inevitably becomes stronger when I'm home in Kerry and I *conduct* myself 'like an Irish person', perhaps in the way I talk amongst my peers, the self-deprecating jokes I make, how I use slang, whatever. But regardless of all that, I can tell you that the question 'What are you?' has followed me around for years. It's a horrible question in which the person who asks it isn't actually interested in my occupation, my religion or my gender. Because I come from a white family, the stranger (they are usually strangers) who asks this question wishes to know me only in the context of my ethnicity and that, my friend, is racism. And when you judge or interact with someone and treat them differently specifically because of the colour of their skin or their ethnic origins, and primarily with negative consequences for that person, that is also racism.

Don't get me wrong, I have no problem with an interest in my birth heritage but it's *why* they're interested which tends to infuriate me. Their asking me, 'Where are you really from?' rarely speaks to an interest in Vietnam itself, the cultural differences, the stories, or traditions. All these strangers care about is my physical appearance – nothing deeper than how I look. And this is also about our obsession with labels and being able to categorise someone to satisfy a limited understanding of the world. People are not keywords, tags or hashtags! 'Where are you really from?' is called an innocent question but it is the opposite of curiosity.

Most of the time the conversation never leads anywhere. One taxi driver proudly exclaimed while I was sitting in the front seat, 'I love the Tiger Beer from your country!' Ugh! I politely explained that Tiger Beer is from Singapore but I am not. This led to a super awkward silence which I was secretly delighted about because I didn't have to deal with any more 'banter'.

Setting aside the law, or being born here, or not being born here, or having parents from here or the multiple reasons why someone is in Ireland, true self-identification is something that comes down to the person themself. Because we can never know the struggles a person has been through to reach their 'identity' nor indeed if a person is still struggling, we must listen and ask kind and respectful questions. Something important to remember when *curiosity* takes a hold of you.

> *Education must be in tune with changes in society*
> **Caithfidh an t-oideachas bheith ag teacht le hathruithe sa tsochaí**

I know I'm Irish and it's something I'm extremely proud to be. I also know I'm not Irish-Vietnamese; I have Vietnamese heritage and I'll be forever grateful to my birth mother for bringing me into this world. But my mother is Noreen and my grandfather was Paddy, and I'm a Kerrywoman and a Gaeilgeoir first and foremost.

I would love for us to set aside physical appearance and be motivated by something deeper, like an interest in the culture or history of a place. So, ask yourself this: if you find yourself wanting to ask a stranger where they are really from, why are you asking?

> *I stand squarely against racism*
> **Tá mé go dubh i gcoinne**
> **an chiníochais**

By now, I have a strong armour and a resilience built up, and I use it ... everyday. It took strength to report the assault, but I would encourage you to do the same if you are ever the survivor of racism. No matter how small or mild the incident, racism is racism and by putting pressure on those in power to treat it as that, we can hope that it will be taken more seriously. It was that boy's attack on me that made me stronger and it galvanised my feelings about my Irish identity. It also gifted me with a new layer of sassiness which I now use in my comebacks all the time (especially when I get the chance to comeback in Irish!).

If you've never been the subject of racism you can count yourself lucky, but you have a responsibility to those who have to recognise this as a privilege and to support them. Remember how utterly alone I felt on that crowded Dublin street. If anyone around me had offered just a bit of kindness that day, together we could have changed the dynamic and I would have felt less isolated.

*An act of kindness*
**Gníomh cineálta**

Since that day, I've learned to use my Irish in truly brilliant and unexpected ways. It has saved me many a time! Once, and this always makes me grin, I was on a crowded Luas heading towards Heuston Station when one lad bellowed at me that there were too many 'Chinese cunts' in this country and that all they were good for were takeaways. I smiled, tilted my head to one side and without moving a muscle said:

'Gabh mo leithscéal?' (Excuse me?)

In absolute disgust, he told me to stop speaking 'fucking Chinese' and I had to stop myself laughing out loud. An older woman nearby seemed to be smothering the same kind of amusement.

'Oh, nach dtuigeann tú mé?' (Oh, don't you understand me?) I asked, feigning concern.

Well, he looked at me as if I could have been speaking any sort of dirty 'foreign' language and appeared visibly annoyed that he couldn't understand me. My body filled with glee and I smiled brightly back at him. I had shut him up.

# From Pastimes to Full-time

It has taken me a while to get to where I am today: a full-time freelancer working in online media and a prolific Irish-language online streamer. My journey to self-employment has not been a straight one and along the way I've tackled depression, boredom, unemployment and social expectations. But these hurdles have only helped me to take control of my working life and in overcoming them I have found ways to reinforce my own boundaries, both professional and personal. Taking the risks, putting myself out there and being true to myself have brought me all sorts of unexpected and delightful surprises. This book is just one those consequences.

In school, I never thought self-employment would be a viable option, as it was sold to us as a risky way to try to make a living. And in my naivety I guess I thought I would be content working the nine-to-five office job. Later, after college, everyone I knew in office positions reinforced that attitude towards work. Yes, I pursued steady jobs and what I believed to be a 'normal' career path, working for someone else, but all the while I was naturally wired for exploration, diversity and entertainment. Ultimately, I found being in an office all day drained my mental health and I felt stifled by a monotonous and an anti-creativity system.

In the jobs that I held during the three years after college, I felt physically weighed down by depression. I began to cry more and stressed about the smallest of things. After a year of unemployment and a severe bout of depression in 2015, I was finally offered another office-based job. I bawled my eyes out at my kitchen table. Finally, I had a job again! And I would be glad of it this time. But six months in, I was depressed once more and in a position I hated. I was angry and sad all the time. I was confused and it was painful to try and wade through those feelings. I didn't know what I wanted to do with my life. I spent many months mulling over my options and finally decided that what I was going through was not worth sacrificing my mental health for. One of the most important questions that I asked myself in deciding whether to go solo was: how can I build all of my passions into my career? I was finally wondering if I could make my love for radio, the internet, journalism, video games and Irish work for me. And in answering those questions, I am certain now that taking the leap away from secure, well-paid, office jobs into the freelance world was what saved me from depression.

*Don't put work before your
mental health*
**Ná chuir an obair roimh do
mheabhairshláinte**

So, I said 'goodbye' to all that and said 'hello' to self-employment. Similar to my college years when I juggled radio, newspaper and online work, I would work on a variety of projects that I was interested in, choosing my own hours and taking control of my work life. I had no idea if I would succeed or if I had made the *right* decision but the most important thing to me was that I had made *a* decision and that brought me great physical, mental and emotional relief. I knew it wasn't going to be easy but my career would be diverse and I've worked steadily ever since on contract work between newswriting, social media marketing and travel writing. I work from home mostly and often work longer hours to hustle for the next job. I've had to learn to become an excellent time manager. I may never be the richest person in the world, but I get exceptional value and diversity out of the different jobs that I do. I have worked in the newsroom of *Lonely Planet*; on national marketing campaigns and social media for restaurants. And

I've even been able to work while on my holidays, creating video content while in Panama and working for TG4 from Vietnam. More and more, from my perspective, the future looks freelance. Companies too, big and small, are catching on. Yes, the hunt for work isn't for everyone but that's what keeps me on the ball, and I see more and more of my peers jumping into this world. I guess I've come of working age in a world where anything can be turned into work. And like the Irish language and County Kerry, one of my first loves in this life has to be video games.

I've happily lost countless days and nights to video games. It was when I was still at primary school that I discovered *Final Fantasy Mystic Quest* on the Super Nintendo Entertainment System (SNES) and *Pokémon* on my Gameboy Colour. I was totally entranced by these worlds. Like the fantasy books I was reading, the games transported me into parts of my imagination that I didn't know existed. I was hooked for life.

The nineties were peak *Pokémon* years and even in our Gaelscoil battles took place *as Gaeilge* in the schoolyard. We connected our Gameboys with a flimsy cable and scattered *Pokémon* cards on the ground. Then during the week I'd head over to a friend's house where we'd spend hours in role playing games (RPGs), sharing the controller. Then I moved firmly into the PlayStation camp, *Final Fantasy* being my favourite series of all time. My grandad was extremely unimpressed by my dedication to the controller. Video games were and still are a form of escapism for me. There can be the misconception that games are a solitary activity, but I've never found that to be the case. The schoolyard was where we shared a lot of tips and when I had friends over playing the PlayStation there was no truer example of 'sharing is caring'. This is still the case today as an adult, where many of my closest friends are those who I have played video games with online. These days we chat to each other via our headsets and we're not just friends playing games, we're a team.

The joy and fulfilment they had always given me made it clear that video games needed to be a part of my working life. Ireland has produced many top-tier games entertainers, making their mark on the world, and I wanted to be a part of that, even if I could only be a drop in that pixelated ocean. *Cén fáth nach?* (Why not?)

In 2017, I signed up to broadcast on a website called Twitch and so began my video game streaming journey. Twitch is a live-streaming video platform that focuses primarily on video game live-streaming, eSports competitions, creative content for artists and live podcasts. If you've ever watched any sports match on television, it's the same concept except you're watching video games and you can interact with the players. I play video games and people watch my reaction as I play them (or I draw, sing or paint live in front of an audience). But because it's live, people can ask me questions and I can answer them back in real time. Essentially, I'm an entertainer, performing live for people and keeping them company. I work for tips and monthly subscribers. Many viewers prefer it because it feels like a more personal experience and is therefore more special for them than traditional video-gaming. In 2018, Twitch had 2.2 million monthly broadcasters and 15 million daily active users worldwide. That's a lot of eyes!

When I live-stream (I dedicate between eight and twelve bilingual hours each week to it), I do so as my alter ego Yunitex. (My name is a combination of two *Final Fantasy* characters which I'll leave hardcore fans to guess.) I have a planned schedule and go live to the public at set times each week. It's exactly like a television schedule but my show isn't scripted and I think this spontaneity and improvisation makes the concept inviting and it's why people tune into me every week.

I began by streaming in English but quickly discovered there was absolutely no one streaming in Irish, so, of course, I seized the opportunity. It felt important to give others the chance to hear Irish in an unexpected environment, outside of the classroom, and hopefully, giving them a fresh perspective on their own pastime. I hoped that by streaming *as Gaeilge* it would encourage others to do the same. This was exactly the kind of change and opportunity Mom meant when she encouraged me to think of a career through Irish. I was finally being the change I had wanted to see.

Since September 2018, two evenings a week, I stream bilingually in Irish and English and once a week I stream *as Gaeilge* only. As an independent content producer and community manager, my focus is on building a community. If there are any changes to my schedule I announce them in advance on my social media. And my 'studio' is my couch at home so it's as casual as they come!

> A generation reared on computer games
> **Glúin a tógadh le cluichí ríomhaireachta**

Those who tune into my Irish-language streams can interact with me on the chat tool and I acknowledge them live in Irish. So, right from the off, my audience is engaged and part of the gaming experience. My generation consumes and classifies entertainment differently to the one before; video games are considered culture. The people who tune into my streams are there for a few different reasons: they're fellow-gamers who were searching for Irish people on Twitch and came across me accidentally; they've spotted me talking about my stream on Twitter and they've popped in to watch out of curiosity or they want to use what Irish they have and listen to the sounds of the language. And what's great is that I can cater to all of them at the same time! Because I can't see their faces, but they can see mine, it takes the pressure off the viewers and their levels of Irish. If they're nervous about their Irish they can observe and listen to me. But if they do want to say something, they have the time to formulate sentences, using a dictionary if they need to. This variety of interactions and competence is of the utmost importance to me in fostering a friendly Irish-language environment within my Twitch community. Twitch is still, in 2019, underused for Irish-language content, despite the potential of its huge audiences.

*Broadcasting on Twitch gladdens my heart*
**Cuireann sé gliondar ar mo chroí nuair a chraolaim ar Twitch!**

By contrast, two of the biggest games in the world are now available to play in the Irish language. *PlayerUnknown's Battlegrounds* (*PUBG*), the popular battle royale shooter, was designed by an Irishman from Kildare, Brendan Greene. It has sold more than 50 million copies and has over 400 million registered *PUBG* players worldwide. In 2019, an Irish-language version of the game was released and this proves to me that interest in our language is evolving healthily. In the world of gaming I often come across individuals and smaller communities who are making a go of fostering a positive attitude towards Irish, in their own practical ways. One such person is Brian C. Mac Giolla Mhuire, the chief Irish-language translator of the *PUBG* project, whose interest in the language and his work on video games fascinated me. Brian is actually Canadian and began learning Irish in university. Prior to that he had had only limited interaction with the language. As he was learning Irish he was dismayed at how few practical resources he could access in Canada, especially ones that would inform his love of gaming. When he saw a post on r/Gaeilge (a subforum on the social news aggregation and content website Reddit. com) asking for help in translating a game called *0 A.D.*, he thought, 'Why not, let's give it a go!'

His pro-active attitude reminds me a lot of my approach when creating #FrásaAnLae. I know if I had seen that request I would have jumped on it too. Even though Brian will say his Irish isn't stellar, he knew he could help more games be translated while improving his own Irish at the same time. Win-win! It was from his work on *0 A.D.* that he stumbled upon a group that was translating for other extremely popular games, *Minecraft* and *PUBG*.

The translation of *PUBG* took approximately three months; its word count approaches 33,000. I see a project like this and I know I would love to have done something cool like this in school. Gaming has a lot of repeated elements, so the meanings of words would have stuck in my brain. Plus, I'd have been working within a subject I love!

Irish is now a built-in language in *PUBG*, and I think this is a brilliant achievement. I love that Brian worked on the Irish translation of a world-famous game for the craic and because he loves Irish so much. He's now considering larger projects like *The Witcher*, *Total War* or a *Paradox* game, but for these colossal translations he'd need years and a whole lot of help. Hey Brian, I'm totally game!

---

*Don't let the opportunity pass you by*
**Ná lig an deis tharat**

---

Like virtual Lego, players can build and create anything they want in *Minecraft*. It's a video game fuelled entirely by the imagination of its players. Believe it or not, despite my creative streak, I'm pretty rubbish at it, but it has helped me practice words like *fardal* (inventory), *pointí beochta* (health points) and *masla an mhála tae* (teabagging), quite essential gaming terms! *Minecraft* is played by approximately 91 million people every month and its very existence in the Irish language gives me hope.

The availability of these globally successful video games in Irish reinforces my belief in the importance of a diversity of activities for any language community, be it video games, music, movies or television shows. If we don't have this kind of varied and contemporary material, we're forced back to the same old stuff like the school curriculum. A lack of new and evolving material can hinder a language's progress and survival. It's up to all of us, not just people like Brian, to be pro-active and positive in our engagement with Irish. That means that some of us will just create things in Irish, in niches or in the mainstream even if there's no immediate promise of pay-off. When I first came to Twitch there were no regular streamers creating content in the Irish language and that's exactly why I leapt at it. Right now, I am the only person in the whole world who streams on Twitch in the Irish language on a weekly basis. Twitch is the 26th most popular website in the entire world and over 15 million people watch streamers like me every day. The scale and reach of this 'niche' world is astounding. It means so much to me now to be working in this environment as this is exactly the kind of content I would have devoured when I was younger. Did I ever think that I would be a success on Twitch? *Seans dá laghad!* (No way!) But with my dedication to this growing part of contemporary culture, I have discovered good things come to those who think outside of the mainstream.

> *Her true passion is video games*
> **Is sna físchluichí atá a croí agus
> a hanam**

I'm constantly astounded by the creativity I see from those who decide to just do it. Ciara Ní É's slam poetry night sessions REIC and the Pop-Up Gaeltachtaí hosted by Peadar Ó Caomhánaigh and Osgur Ó Ciardha inspire me to do more. Like #FrásaAnLae, Twitch and my live streaming are now just parts of my working life and I'm better for them.

They've given me the opportunity to connect with people *because* of Irish not *despite* it and regardless of our backgrounds and beliefs. I had nothing to lose by venturing into online streaming and everything to gain. If you had asked me in school what job I'd have in the future, there'd be no way I would have said 'freelance content creator'; those words would have been totally foreign to me and my peers. And if he could see me now, I think Grandad would find it amusing that I'm doing all of this business *as Gaeilge*. I'm grateful to be part of the Irish-language generation for whom technology, opportunity and 'normal' work have changed drastically. These developments in the way we work and the way we play have allowed me to adapt my life in support of a better state of mind, fuelled by my passions. You can't wait around to see if others will do something. You're the one who must take the plunge.

*It's time you got off your butt*
**Nach mithid duit do thóin a bhogadh**

# #WeAreIrish

I have these moments sometimes, when I can't shake off a new idea, what I like to call a 'notion'. By April 2017, I was digitally fluent and was often using Twitter to talk about Irish identity. After a series of threads musing on what it was like for me as a person of colour in Ireland, I got the notion to do something much bigger. I really wanted to explore the definition of Irishness in this day and age and what it meant to me and my peers. Deep down, I wanted to challenge the idea of what an Irish person is supposed to look and sound like. And despite all my talk on Twitter, I knew words could only do so much. My notion called for some creativity and courage. For the time being, though, while I was researching it, I kept my 'diversity project' under wraps, and because I had a good and professional reputation elsewhere on the internet, I decided this should be a social media-only project.

See, for a long time I'd been thinking: were there other people like me, who didn't have the 'look of the Irish', people who were mixed race, adopted, non-white or who were often mistaken as non-Irish? And had they been targeted because they had the 'wrong' colour skin? These challenges were not for me alone to talk about. Unbelievably, even though I had always been open online about my experiences of racism there and in the real world, it just hadn't yet occurred to me to reach out to other people in Ireland who had experienced the same intrusive questioning about their identity as I had. I didn't set out to be an activist, but by starting my diversity project, I suddenly realised I could help amplify other people. I couldn't do it on my own, I needed their help. So, I sent out a request on Facebook and Twitter to take part in my project.

**Úna-Minh (is my first name) Caomhánach**
@unakavanagh
Request please: my fellow Irish men and women who don't look 'stereotypically Irish' – could you message me please? RTs welcome : )
1:06PM • Apr 15, 2017
**313** Retweets                              **140** Likes

Soon a collage of profile pictures appeared. They were faces from all walks of life, of all ages, who had one thing in common: they all identified as Irish. There was a mix of white people and people of colour and as I pulled their pictures together, I found myself emotional that they were so willing to take part in my project. All this time, all these people were right there, just a tweet away. There was a woman whose father was Zambian and her mother was Irish; a man whose parents were from Hong Kong and he was born in Ireland; a non-binary Irish-born Chinese person. RTÉ's Rick O'Shea, Irish comedian Tara Flynn, writer Sarah Maria Griffin and screenwriter Stefanie Preissner were allies who amplified the message. I was so delighted to hear from them all! They shared their stories with me freely, of how they were constantly asked where they were 'really' from and I discovered that many of them were also Irish-language speakers! They told me how they had been challenged, on the regular, about their 'Irishness' and how they had received ugly and racist abuse because of what they claimed to be.

Born and bred in Belfast. Half-Indian and half-Irish and constantly get asked where I am REALLY from? I consistently have to justify that I am in fact from Belfast. Been called 'exotic', 'ethnic looking', 'half-cast' all as 'compliments'. Also men in particular love to guess where I'm from even after I've insisted I'm from Belfast. Both my brothers get comments too but nowhere as many as me and not as invasive. Ninety per cent of comments come from men hitting on me...'

—

I'm adopted, my birth father was Maltese. Growing up I was nicknamed 'cocopop' or the 'n-word' because I was dark skinned. I got so freaked that I stopped going into the sun for years!

—

Where are you from? But where were you born? But where are you really from? I don't even think I look that 'foreign' but apparently, I look foreign enough for that to be a conversation starter. Every. Single. Time. I'm half-Spanish, my Mum is from there but I was born in Dublin. I've never lived in Spain...

—

I'm half-Indian and Irish and for some reason I always get asked what part of Greece or Spain I'm from. Someone once said to my mam that, regarding myself and my sister, that she was lucky to adopt sisters

Even though everyone's stories were different, there were parts of them that struck me straight away. For one, 'Where are you really from?' the absolute bane of my life. Discovering that I wasn't so alone after all delighted me beyond measure. From the profile pictures these contributors gifted me, I was able to create something beautiful with their faces, a collage that spoke to the beauty and diversity of Irishness in the twenty-first century. With seventy-four faces gathered together in the one, media-friendly format, the #WeAreIrish hashtag was born on Twitter and it quickly became a shortcut for celebrating diversity. The replies, retweets and likes that it gathered naturally moved the campaign away from looks alone. Although I was the one who needed the help from others, ultimately it was a better realised project for what the Twittersphere gave back to me.

> #WeAreIrish
> **#IsÉireannaighMuid**

When I shared the collage on Facebook and Twitter, the reaction was immense. It prompted another flurry of stories from all over Ireland and abroad, from Irish people who had such love for their culture. To date, my collage has been seen over 140,000 times on Twitter and engaged with by over 13,000 users, meaning people looking at it, clicking on it and looking at the image up close. It received over 1600 likes and 600 retweets. There were hundreds of replies to my tweets, retweeted responses to the collage and the hashtag. Facebook comments, direct messages and emails came in from people I'd never met but who instinctively knew what I was trying to do. #WeAreIrish had kick-started a long-awaited conversation highlighting diversity in Ireland.

**Dean Van Nguyen**
@deanvannguyen
I am an Irishman. A proud, half-white, half-Asian, Irishman. I pity those that upsets. They're sufferers of a disease of the mind #weareirish

**Philip O'Connor**
@philipoconnor
Níl aon *áit* i mo *Éirinn* do chiníochas, leithcheal,
fuath ná Twitter-amadán gan ainm.
#weareirish

*(There's no place in my Ireland for racism, discrimination*
*or hate or any Twitter fool without a name)*

Very quickly, #WeAreIrish began to feel like a bona fide online social movement with an overwhelmingly positive response. I focussed on these but there was a dark side too, of course, and soon the racists and trolls were out in force flipping appalling phrases at me. Many of the worst of them have since been deleted or removed by Twitter.

**Minority Report**
@Minority_Member
Replying to @brianmcdonagh and @unakavanagh
You should RT this when your towns are overrun
with mud people and your daughters are being
packed raped in the streets. #weareirish

—

Shitty brown parasites.

—

Stop trying to be us you fucking cunt. I don't
staple my eyes slanty and say I'm Chinese, do I?

—

Fuck out of my country ya daft cunt

—

Harro maybe iv I spell name in Irwish I'll become
rike rem


In the interest of accuracy and posterity, I purposefully have not censored the spelling in their tweets
because this is the reality for people of colour who
put themselves out there, loud and proud. Obscenity,
poor grammar and spelling are synonymous with
these trolls and I have no interest in protecting their
ignorance. The thing to know about trolls is, if they
are not bots, they are entrenched in their views. Their
goal is to upset the user, it's not even to change a
user's mind. And absolutely no amount of discussion (respectful or otherwise) is going to change the
mind of a troll. You cannot reason with a troll and
it's a waste of precious energy, time and headspace
to try to. So, instead, I try to lighten the tone, and
in this instance I began to donate one euro to the
European Network Against Racism for every negative tweet I got from one particular fool. They made
some moolah off of his idiocy and that troll has since
been suspended from Twitter. Success! Once again,
I was turning repulsive actions into humour and
positive results. And I was, importantly, protecting

myself from the relentless nastiness and exposure of the internet.

> *It was a pathetic attempt*
> **Lagiarracht amach is amach
> a bhí ann**

Just a few days after the hashtag went out, the slew of racist and trolling tweets that followed told me instantly that the hashtag itself was being targeted. And, Janey Mac, did the trolls love piling on comments, which caused a bombardment of tweets, which in turn caused my comments and account to trend on Twitter. Unfortunately, they were also trending in another place online, one of the scariest corners of the wild and weird web. 4chan.org is an image-based forum where all of its users are anonymous and approximately 70 per cent of them are male. Their anonymity creates a space that is unfiltered, a place where users can post whatever they want without owning their content. Why worry about 4chan.org, you might ask. Well, it is the absolute opposite of a safe space and, in my opinion, a cesspit of hate. Things get dark very quickly. Terrifyingly, around 22 million people use the website each month and 42 billion users have visited the site since its inception in 2004. The 4chan community is known for being provocative for the sake of controversy, as some of its users are hooked on the quick high that comes from trolling some unsuspecting innocent. In a clever move, their trolls had scanned through my Twitter timeline and downloaded my image for Photoshopping into memes, disturbing scenarios and racist slogans. By going viral, #WeAreIrish had attracted the wrong kind of attention. And once you are trending on 4chan.org you are going to get a deluge of notifications. I soon discovered that their corrupted images of me were tweeted attached to #WeAreIrish. But I counteracted this hateful imagery by asking my followers to simply tweet with the hashtag and we were able to flood Twitter with the opposite of hate.

**Úna-Minh (is my first name) Caomhánach**
@unakavanagh
Racism, discrimination and hate have no place in my Ireland #WeAreIrish
9:02PM • Apr 20, 2017
**81** Likes

*Don't feed the trolls!*
**Ná beathaítear na troill!**

Even though 4chan.org and the actions of its users are just a tiny, niche cavity of the web, I was determined to show followers – and if I could, the folks at Twitter itself – that the trolls were out there, and it was possible to combat them. I wanted to say, loud and clear, that Twitter didn't need to be like 4chan to feed itself. The support that I received for #WeAreIrish proved to me that my audience (nearly 12,000) were far more interested in stamping out trolls than being in their circle of animosity.

Sure, I'm well aware that for the meme-makers, the proud racists and the closet racists, it doesn't matter that I have an Irish passport. Nor does it matter I've lived here all of my life. I'm just too brown for them. And they think they can upset me by bringing this up every time. It's their only line of offence. According to them, I am 'anti-white', 'anti-native-Irish' and I'm committing 'genocide' on the Irish people by stealing their identities. So far these comments only make me snort out in laughter.

> *The coward has many deaths*
> **Is iomaí bás ag an meatachán**

Now, I know, I know, you may say, 'ignore them, block them', but let's remember the drip, drip effect of racism and how much easier it is to think turning a blind eye will make racism magically disappear. When racism is not a thing that happens to you over and over again, blanket statements like that deflect from the real issue at hand. Racism is rampant. Even if I can take it, I know there are lots of other people who look like me or feel like me who can't. And I guess I feel a responsibility to stand up against trolls and racism on their behalf. Call me foolish, or call me an ally, your choice. I was already pretty tech-savvy and I knew that I had do some self-care in the aftermath but the temptation to check every single message as my phone buzzed was chipping away at my energy and attention levels. I will admit that as these hate messages piled up – behind anonymous accounts – I began to question whether starting #WeAreIrish had been worth it.

*A clear conscience is the best pillow*
**Coinsias glan an adhairt is fearr**

So, having begun a grassroots social media diversity campaign that went viral all by myself, I had to make the tough decision to pull away from Twitter for a while. 'Doxxers' had made an appearance, direct messages threatening to reveal all my personal details online. The act of 'doxxing' is the attempt to release online a person's private information, for example, your Facebook account login, your home address or your phone number. Creepy, right? Very often, these are empty threats but because I knew that I had been a subject on 4chan.org and because of the size of their user base, I took some deep breaths and switched off my phone to spend hours away from social media. This kind of online exposure has been known to destroy gentler folk. I knew I needed to protect myself, despite having learned to handle my own presence on the internet with flair and sassiness rather than anger.

Take, for example the case of 'Barry' who wrote me an email in February 2017, just two months before I created #WeAreIrish. It was addressed to me personally as well as the *Irish Independent*.

*Although it is wrong for anyone to be abused for being non-Irish, I would ask you to consider the other side of racism, I would ask you to consider how the people of Ireland are being affected culturally and demographically by mass migration. I would ask you to consider how when someone who is clearly not Irish claims to be Irish, how this affects us as people. If there are no parameters to being Irish, if anyone can claim to [be]*

*Irish, then being Irish becomes meaningless. To make the Irish people a meaningless people is the height of racism and a crime against humanity. If we allow ourselves to become a meaningless people, our extinction is not far away.*

*You can only be Irish if you are a product of the Irish environment, this is biological. The Irish people are a genetically unique and distinct people, this is confirmed by genetic research.*

*'DNA testing through the male Y chromosome has shown that Irish males have the highest incidence of the haplogroup 1 gene in Europe. While other parts of Europe have integrated contiuous [sic] waves of new settlers from Asia, Ireland's remote geographical position has meant that the Irish gene-pool has been less susceptible to change. The same genes have been passed down from parents to children for thousands of years.' Source [his source was an article on apparent Irish blood origins].*

*Please join together and stop the gradual demographic genocide of the Irish people.*
*Kind Regards,*
*Barry*

Now, I know what you're thinking. Firstly, scarlet for ya, Barry, I nearly died of boredom reading that. And, secondly, ah here, what an absolute dope. And I'd agree with you on both points. This wasn't the first and nor will it be the last email of this kind I will receive.

*Ach tá an saol róghearr agus is bean ana-ghnóthach mé* (But life's too short and I'm a very busy woman)! Barry, I reckoned, has the personality of a spoon.

> He's a snide little gobshite
> **Slíomadóir suarach atá ann**

I mulled it over. Not his message, mind you, but whether I should respond to him. I decided that even though he was definitely a gombeen with no life outside the internet, he was also a gombeen that I needed to put back in his *bosca*. So, I called upon my secret weapon – I responded to him in Irish. Then, I turned to my other secret weapon and I shared our interaction on Twitter:

*Barry,*
*Maidir le do ríomhphost: Is léir go bhfuil tuairimí láidre agat. I ndáil leis an gciníochas a luadh san alt, níl aon 'taobh eile' mar a déarfá. Is mór an trua nach bhfeiceann tú cé chomh cúngaigeanta is atá do 'phointí'.*

*Tá dearcadh lofa, diúltach, duairc ar an saol agat gan aon sonas. Nílimse freagrach as, do mhothúcháin neamhshláine. Níl an locht orm go bhfuil féinmhuinín agam ionam féin (rud nach bhfuil agat is dóigh).*

*Ceapaimse go bhfuil sé go hiomlán truamhéalach gur sheol tú ríomhphost pearsanta chugam chun do chiníochas a chomhfhadú.*

*Mise le meas,*

*Úna-Minh Caomhánach – Ciarraíoch agus Éireannach*

(*Barry,*

*In relation to your email: It's clear that you've strong opinions. But there's no 'other side to racism' as you say. It's a shame that you don't see how narrow-minded your 'points' are.*

*You've a disgusting, negative, depressing outlook on the world without any joy and I'm not responsible for your feelings of insecurity. It's not my problem that I've confidence in myself either (something that you're clearly lacking).*

*I think it's absolutely pathetic that you sent this personal email to me just to reemphasise your racism.*

*Kind regards,*

*Úna-Minh Kavanagh – Kerrywoman and Irishwoman*)

I never received a response, and even if I had, I wouldn't have engaged further. My part was done. After tweeting it I received yet another wave of support from my community which was heart-warming and a boost of energy I needed.

**Hozier**
@Hozier
Replying to @unakavanagh

Glorious hi-five in your direction, incredibly
well handled, Úna. There's some REAL empty
f***ers out there. Hope you're well!

**DublinByMouth: Niamh**
@DublinByMouth
Replying to @unakavanagh
boom. Cur é sin i do phíopa a Bharra.

**Órfhlaith Ní C**
@OrfhlaithNiC
Replying to @unakavanagh
Iontach Úna. Bíodh fios agat go seasann níos mó
daoine leat ná i d'aghaidh. Ní ceart go mbeadh ar dhuine ar bith
plé leis seo.

**Dálaigh**
@Dailigh
Replying to @unakavanagh
Currently no. 1 post for 2017.

Did Barry hope that I'd suddenly change my mind
about my own identity and be, like: 'Oh Jaysis, I'm
desperately sorry. You're right, I'm not an iota bit of
Irish, and you're spot on. I'll pack my bags and head
across the pond. Slán.'

> *Piss off*
> **Bailigh leat**

Each time I've had to deal with trolls online, I've learned a bit more about myself and indeed how I react to things. Where once I would have started a massive row with a pointless back and forth, knowing well they were only trying to get a rise out of me, now that's not my style at all. I still talk about Irish identity and racism on occasion, and I do highlight some of the racist and awful comments that are thrown at me, but these days there's no fight. Instead of being angry when I see trolling or racist tweets, I now feel pro-active. In the most natural way, they fire me up to continue talking about these issues which, in turn, helps me to reach more people with my story. My guiding intention now is that the tweets I share will shatter the naivety that some people still have surrounding racism. So, thank you trolls for making me even more popular!

> *I'm stronger than them*
> **Táimse níos láidre ná iadsan**

True, there are still moments since my tête-à-tête with Barry when I feel frustrated at the lack of acceptance, but it remains important to me to stay positive and to use my influence for good. It really does feel good to help others and that's all I want to do when it comes to my social media activities. When I find myself getting too invested in a troll, trying to suss out what they're up to or if I feel like a massive angry rant would go down well on Twitter, I return to a line in my grandad's funeral appreciation: 'Never become so important that you take yourself too seriously.'

# Better Than One

I love being Irish and bilingual. I've been able to enjoy so many experiences and cultivate long-lasting friendships, sometimes in the most unexpected ways and places. I really do feel like I have double the fun! An ease with one language, such as Irish, often leads to a comfort and sometimes even a fascination with many other languages. That's how it was for me, but I know there are many who will say that they love the idea of having Irish but loathe the reality of learning it. And others are convinced that a foreign language is more 'useful' than Irish in gaining employment and success. However, learning Irish need not exclude you from learning other languages. Because Irish has only ever been good for me, I'm going to show you the benefits of our native tongue as I have experienced them. But first, let's tackle some of the reasons (or, excuses) I often hear for not learning Irish like any other interesting language.

'It's too late for me to learn.' *Sin seafóid!* Nonsense! If you do really want to learn, it's never too late. One friend in his late-thirties went back to Irish because he wanted to send his child to a Gaelscoil and he wanted be able to help her with her homework. Another friend in her twenties set about relearning the language like a project: daily exercises in language apps like Duolingo. This, in turn, gave her greater focus in easing her anxiety and brought her a new-found confidence. Their age doesn't matter to them or their ability to learn, it's what they planned to do with the language that is a motivator. Indeed, those who did learn it at school and who are out of practice are surprised when they understand more than they expected. A pleasant surprise at any age, I'd think.

> *Laziness is a heavy burden*
> **Trom an t-ualach an leisce**

Those who begin language studies at an older age can still achieve fluency levels. And engaging with another language helps your brain to communicate, to recognise new words and to negotiate meaning in problem-solving tasks. My fluency means I am able to transition from one language to another with little or no effort. Though I'm not fluent in more than two languages, I find having Irish has helped me understand and remember words in other languages, for example, French. The word for small church/chapel in French is *chappelle* (sha-pell) and in Irish it is *séipéal* (shay-pale). Similar, no? Tea in French is *thé* (tay) and in Irish it's *tae* (tay). Again, to my ear, they are similar. And what Irish person wouldn't want to learn about tea in multiple languages?! Finally, *mille*, the French word for a thousand is pronounced mee-leh, a bit like the Irish word for a thousand, *míle*. The logic within my bilingual brain helps me learn and differentiate the similarities between these two languages; bilingualism means I have prior learning strategies built into my brain.

> They flip between languages
> effortlessly
> **Bíonn siad ag dul ó theanga
> go teanga gan stró**

Another common complaint goes like this: 'How come, after so many years at school, no one can speak it?' Well, let's consider this: *years* spent learning

Irish actually means *hours* spent learning it. Here is rough estimation of the time spent learning Irish in the average English-speaking secondary school in Ireland. With an average of 167 days in a school year, just under three and a half hours each week are allocated to the Irish language (five classes of forty minutes each). That's about 117 hours per year, and somewhere between 585 and 701 hours over a student's secondary school career (on a five and a six-year cycle and not including half days, sick days, sports days and school tours). Many of my hours of Irish learning were taken up with memorisation of the same content instead of communication skills.

Added to this is the challenge of teaching a language in a finite length of time to students of mixed abilities and interests. *An Triail*, the classic Irish-language play by Máiréad Ní Ghráda which premiered in 1964, has been on the Leaving Certificate curriculum since 2006. I did my Leaving Certificate in 2009 and a fellow I know did his Leaving Certificate in 2019. We were ten years apart, but we studied *An Triail* in the exact same way, learning crib sheets off by heart, with the same notes and interpretations regurgitated year on year. My issue is not with the text itself but the fact that it was the *only* text we both studied, regardless of wider social and cultural developments in the intervening years. It's no wonder students are disillusioned with a language course like Irish when major parts of it remain the same.

I just don't think it's possible for a person to become fluent with an average of just three and a half hours of Irish each week without any 'outside of school' stimulation. The expectations – wrapped up in national pride and ideology – are unrealistic, so it's no surprise to me that many leave school without confidence in the language. It's not unreasonable to expect language learners to have only a basic under-standing of Irish after such a short time. By contrast, those who, like me, spoke and heard Irish constantly at home and attended the Gaeltacht every summer, enjoyed the benefits of 'out of school hours' immer-sion. All students, whatever their level, need diverse and active engagement with a language and if I had my way, they would encounter Irish everywhere!

*Practice brings mastery (i.e. practice makes perfect)*
**Táithí a dhéanann máistreacht**

Then there are the complete naysayers who believe Irish is already over, 'It is a dead language' being a key throwaway statement made in angst. It's usually linked to a lack of interest in the language by young people. Well, the millions of views of Coláiste Lurgan's Irish-language videos on YouTube tell a different story, as do the comments section. A dead language is one *no one speaks*, with no hope of resurrection. But naysayers must be reminded that just because they don't speak it, doesn't mean others don't.

Finally, and possibly the most triggering of moans for Irish speakers is: 'Why don't we learn a useful language instead?' Calling one language more 'useful' than another is not only an insult to the belittled language, it ignores the fact that not all languages are tools for business. The passion for learning a language can take you to tangible usefulness. For many Irish-Americans, learning Irish is 'useful' because it connects them to their ancestors' culture. One of my followers on Twitch, the live-streaming entertainment platform, tells me they're learning Ulster-Irish because their family emigrated from the Gaoth Dobhair Gaeltacht in Donegal. While English is a global language and, these days, a language of trade, there are still many parts of our globalised world where minority and local languages are favoured. When I travel, then, it means I must try a little harder to communicate and, as the speaker of a minority language of my own, I'm okay with that. Not least because gesturing and doing charades often finds me in humorous situations. Once, while stopping in a Vietnamese rural homestay, I needed to explain that I didn't want any chili. I formed an 'X' with my hands, pointed to my red t-shirt and used my hands to make a virtual chili shape, saying 'không cay' which is very poor Vietnamese for 'no hot'. I then started fanning myself and looked a right state, but we all laughed and, hey, I got no chili!

*The benefits of it are clear*
**Is léir na buntáistí a bhaineann leis**

If the privilege of global communication lies with speakers of French, English, Spanish, Arabic or Chinese, then it's on those speakers to not dismiss other languages as useless. When you're in a minority it's exhausting trying to fight for the Irish corner and articles about its 'uselessness' don't help. But I'm also in a majority as an English-speaker and so I have a position and platform to pro-actively seek out speakers and users – online and offline – of the Irish language. We're not in the shadows, you can find us too! My YouTube video playing *Fortnite* in Irish has prompted teachers to reach out me to say they are showing my video in their classes. The Irish language is agile and alive enough to be taught positively and in a modern way.

Your tongue will bring you to Rome
**Tabharfaidh do theanga chun na Róimhe thú**

Have you ever heard a dramatic performance of our national anthem, 'Amhrán na bhFiann', on the mountains of Munnar in India? Just take a moment to imagine what that feels like. Whenever I've travelled and I've told the people I've met that Ireland indeed has her own native tongue, I'm met quite often with a look of complete awe and intrigue. This excites me, I get an absolute thrill out of talking about Irish and sharing the *cúpla focal* (few words) with them. For many of us, Irish will only be experienced through our educational system and I think we often forget that not everyone is familiar with the long and complicated history of our language. When I'm travelling and get asked about the language, I don't meet the put-down mentality that many of us have acquired. It's often only when we leave Ireland that we can see it through the eyes of a foreigner, as a special, minority language.

In 2017, I was invited to represent Ireland at the Kerala Blog Express, an initiative by the Kerala tourism board to use the experiences of travel bloggers to encourage people to visit Kerala. Kerala is an Indian state in the south west of the country, right on the Malabar Coast. It has a population of over 38 million people and two official languages, Malayalam and English. This was my first visit to India and, having received no advance itinerary – we were told by the tourism board that we would experience 'the best of Kerala' – our two-and-a-half week trip felt like a big mystery about to unfold before me. I arrived jet-lagged to the city of Kochi, where the heat blasted in my face and the humidity took over my body. I felt immediately sticky but was over the moon when I was shepherded into an air-conditioned car. I arrived a few days before the official start of the Blog Express and so I had time to attempt to get used to the heat. Spoiler alert: I didn't! Even in my specially chosen linen clothes, I was absolutely melting and my only saviour was the swimming pool.

At the first gathering of bloggers (from twenty-nine different countries) at a hotel in Kochi city, I met Evelyn Ang Loo, a proud Malaysian woman. In a conference room of the hotel, I was surrounded by cameras, journalists and people of all nationalities. The bloggers were Peruvian, British, South African, Indonesian, American and Romanian as well as twenty-three other nationalities. It kind of felt like a gathering of the United Nations! Each of us had to take to the stage in front of cameras and talk about our blog and what we were looking forward to in Kerala. Nearly everyone was bilingual and, though English was our common language, everyone was excited to share part of their culture and language. Evelyn had a beautiful smile and I liked her immediately. As one of the older people on the blogger trip, she wasn't afraid to kick-start a conversation and she came over to me to introduce herself. My stress around new people was probably accentuated being so far from home, but Evelyn's friendly demeanour calmed me instantly. She became like a supportive big sister during the trip, looking out for everyone in the Kerala Blog Express group. Evelyn recounted stories of her family and her love for Malaysia and her culture. Later, at our inaugural lunch, she showed me how to eat food delicately with just my hands. She took my hand in hers and arranged my fingers into a loose ball-shape and said, 'You just curve and then dip in, lah'. 'Lah', she delightfully explained, is an emphasis in Malay and was an innate part of her identity as a Malaysian woman. While English is a recognised language in Malaysia, Evelyn said she always preferred to use her native tongue when given the choice. While she appreciated that we could communicate to each other in English, the history that came with Malay was far more appealing to her because it was part of her own heritage. I thought it was interesting that this was Evelyn's choice to make, in a country of approximately 137 indigenous languages.

I had the busiest two-and-a-half weeks of my life on the Kerala Blog Express. I floated through the Alappuzha backwaters in a houseboat as the sun beat down on me. I saw Mohiniyattam, the traditional graceful dance of the region, performed by women who were draped in gold. I learned about the efforts of local communities to create more eco-friendly experiences. And throughout, I was eating paneer (an Indian cheese) at every meal. Obviously, I was in heaven. In all of these experiences, one moment stands out in my mind: a hiking and camping trip to Munnar in the Western Ghats. The area was lush green and dotted with tea plantations. Compared with the densely populated cities, Munnar was like a quiet retreat. One evening, our group had a barbeque and bonfire party under the starlight. The food was delicious and plenty of drink was had, but after a while I could feel my eyelids start to droop.

Evelyn and I snuck away from the partying to get an early night's sleep (I get cranky if I don't get at least seven hours). We settled into our tent, keeping an eye out for mosquitos, and began to talk. I told Evelyn about Ireland, its culture and also the language. She was aware of Irish but had never heard it spoken before. She asked for me to say a few words and because talking to her had given me a new found energy, I felt comfortable in obliging her. I didn't want to just give her something common like 'An bhfuil cead agam dul go dtí an leithreas?' or 'Dia dhuit', so I needed a moment to think. Finally I landed on 'Amhrán na bhFiann'. I knew the first verse and chorus off by heart since it was drilled into me during my time working in Coláiste na bhFiann's Gaeltachtaí. The lyrics came easily, the melody lilted through me and, feeling really confident by the end, I finished with a flourish of my hands for effect.

I tell this story for a few reasons. First, I was moved by how proud Evelyn was of her culture and her language and how much she wanted to share it with others. And second, I am still impressed by her genuine interest in our Irish language. She told me that she had worked with a few Irish people over the years in Malaysia, but they weren't fluent in the language. Hearing a part of our national anthem spoken *as Gaeilge* in the flesh was not what she had expected from a trip to Kerala!

> I'll never forget that day
> **Ní dhéanfaidh mé dearmad
> ar an lá sin choíche**

Sadly, Evelyn passed away in tragic circumstances since then, which affected me deeply. But her memory lives on in my heart. I long to spend more time with her but remember that this moment together in the mountains of Munnar will have to be enough. With so many indigenous languages in Malaysia, I felt she understood what it felt like to be protective of one such as Irish and why it was good to share it. When I think about the fun and positivity of using Irish in unexpected places, Evelyn is the first to come to mind. Because of her willingness to simply listen and understand, my conversations with Evelyn about the Irish language were all positive, even though she didn't speak Irish or have any intention of learning it. That meant a lot to me and still does.

Frustration and the attendant shame can prevent us from relearning a language. Many people I speak to about their lack of interest in relearning Irish also speak of a deep sense of failure that they didn't learn it the first time. Then there are those who feel the moment for relearning has passed. And this is sometimes accompanied by a nostalgia for how their grandparents spoke Irish; the 'I would've loved to learn' attitude. All of these reasons and excuses make for a very emotionally confusing status quo. But I say again, *seafóid*, don't be ashamed, failure is part of the journey! And by sweeping aside these emotions and simply deciding that it's never too late to learn, anyone can be gently prompted to start again.

One of my greatest bugbears is the representation of Irish on some media platforms and how their open comments sections degenerate into a sparring war between speakers, non-speakers and trolls. Peig Sayers and 'It's a dead language anyway' get trotted out and, at the very least, create jealousy and insecurity amongst speakers as well as enthusiasts who are still deciding to become learners. Trolls, in particular, thrive on inciting hatred and division, showing disdain for any sort of discussion or reminder that Irish is actually spoken and celebrated by some of us. In my experience of these online skirmishes, those who have no intention of learning Irish are often the loudest and most vocal in their opinion of it as a waste of space. They also believe *Gaeilgeoirí* see themselves as superior or 'more Irish' than everyone else. This simply isn't true. I use the language because I love it, not because it gives me extra 'Irish' brownie points. For my grandad Irish was a natural form of communication. He came from a simple and poor upbringing, and Irish gave him joy and harmless pride. All these articles do is reinforce a negative image of the language, devoid of a balance of opinion. Over the years I have learned to resist the pull of this nonsense and instead use my online profile to share the best of what Irish has to offer. A note to those who are tempted to fall into the comment sections: beware of those who thrive on whinging. They don't deserve your energy or time.

> *Stop your whingeing*
> **Fág uait an chnáimhseáil**

Like any kind of gathering of humans, particularly in internet comment sections, there will always be a minority who will behave obnoxiously towards the rest. But don't let these people deter you from trying to learn a new language.

I'd like to help you see that your Irish can be reclaimed. With a bit more effort you can separate it from all of the mixed up feelings you gained while in school. For example, relearning French is a challenge for me because I want to go beyond the standard 'Bonjour, ça va?' and converse about video games. I have to work harder to find the learning materials and the opportunities to use the language in this way, but my determination keeps me motivated.

The key to language learning for me is immersion. Contrary to popular belief, that doesn't mean you must pack your bags, nab a hundred things from IKEA and move to the Gaeltacht. Immersion starts with baby steps. Decide how much you want to learn Irish and then prioritise it. You must want it enough. And like many things that are new and unfamiliar it can feel like a sacrifice in the beginning ('I could be watching "RuPaul's Drag Race" instead'), but the same could be said of anything you set your mind to. There is truth to the old cliché of practice makes perfect.

*Your efforts won't go unrecognised*
**Tabharfar aitheantas do do chuid iarrachtaí**

Jumping into a new language can be daunting, but attitude is everything! One of the most interesting tips that I've received is that if you focus on being understood and getting a result and not on being grammatically correct all the time, then you're halfway there. And I find when I travel (as a travel blogger, I do that a lot!) making that extra effort to be understood feels great because the people I meet appreciate me trying. Backpacking around Panama, I made a conscious decision to use as little English as possible as I saw the trip as an opportunity for full immersion. I decided to prioritise my Spanish learning while on holiday! (Did I mention I'm also learning Spanish?) Every morning I would practice my Spanish using language apps like Memrise, and then throughout the day I listened to Spanish-English bilingual podcasts. It was a lot of craic! I was definitely butchering my Spanish pronunciation (did I mention I'm also learning Spanish?), but I survived and had one of the best holidays of my life. By contrast, I know many Irish learners who spend hours with the language online and in textbooks but are then too afraid to speak it for fear they make a mistake. There is no improvement without the odd mistake every now and then. I really don't see the point of learning a language if you don't practice it. We have an opportunity as Irish speakers and learners to share a special experience surrounded by sound people. Even if you can't meet in person, Skype, Discord or Google Hangouts can be a great free way to reach out to an Irish-speaker. Practice with like-minded people and you won't be afraid to make a hames of it. As learners in a community, know that you are not alone and that there are plenty of resources. The book you hold in your hand right now is just one of them!

With a second language like Irish, we are open to potentially twice the amount of information, media and texts. *Game of Thrones* (*Cluiche na Corónach*), *Harry Potter and the Philosopher's Stone* (*Harry Potter agus an Órchloch*), *The Hobbit* (*An Hobad*) have all been published in Irish; extremely popular video games like *Overwatch*, *PUBG* and *Minecraft* feature Irish and there are even rappers who exclusively make new music in Irish: shout out to Belfast rappers KNEECAP!

Irish opens me up to new experiences that I wouldn't have if I was monolingual. And the Irish of twenty-first century Ireland isn't as archaic as some people might think. The language is yours for the owning; it just takes *beagáinín* (a little) more effort.

# #FrásaAnLae

In 2011, I was working with WorldIrish.com, an online community for the Irish or anyone who has an affinity with Ireland, aimed at harnessing the power of existing social networks while deepening the relationship of users to the Irish experience, across culture, arts, sports, media, business and science. There, I started a daily post called *Téarma an Lae* (Term of the Day) that was published simultaneously on several social media platforms. The reaction to this series was extremely positive and, though the daily production of it became slow and cumbersome (I have since mastered the art of regular and simultaneous posting), the act of sharing something daily *as Gaeilge* appealed enormously to me. In time, I moved on to other projects and commitments, building my profile online, and it would be seven years before I returned to an online series of any kind.

It wasn't until one dark night in December 2018, when I was flicking through the online *Fócloir* that I thought to myself: 'What kind of Irish-language content would easily draw people in?' 'What do I enjoy creating?' and 'What publishing system could I put in place so it wouldn't be a chore?' The internet, and certainly social media, had drastically changed since my days at WorldIrish.com, and perhaps ongoing series and campaigns had become more sophisticated and effective since. I thought about updating *Téarma an Lae* for an equally evolved audience. I was inspired by the great Irish writer, Samuel Beckett, who wrote: 'Ever tried. Ever failed. No matter. Try again. Fail again. Fail better.' This time around I wanted to show that phrases in the Irish language go far beyond 'Póg mo thóin' and 'An bhfuil cead agam dul go dtí an leithreas?' and I wanted to have some craic doing it.

For short, snappy, humorous and curious phrases in Irish, Twitter seemed to me a natural home. I had sent out 80,000 tweets by then (a shocking number, I know!) so I could tweet blindfolded! I discovered that both *Frása an Lae* (Phrase of the Day) and *Focal an Lae* (Word of the Day) were hashtags that had previously been used, but not daily and not consistently as I intended. I found it very easy to feed my tweets with my *Fócloir* (dictionary) by my side, checking single words here and there. But *frása* (phrase) would allow me to bring just a little more personality to the series, an irresistible approach for this digital pup!

I sent the first #FrásaAnLae tweet on 11 December 2018 and it was a cheeky one. Lord only knows who I was ranting about:

**Úna-Minh (is my first name) Caomhánach**
@unakavanagh
Today's Irish prhase of the day is: cé hé an stail asail sin?
Meaning: who's that asshole?
#FrásaAnLae #Gaeilge
6:07 PM • Dec 11, 2018
**32** Retweets                    **126** Likes

For no good or philosophical reason other than the fact that it made me laugh, #FrásaAnLae began funny and sweary. And boy did this resonate with people. I was astounded by the immediate interest from those who spoke Gaeilge as well as those who were just curious about the language. And even though I had a much greater online following in late 2018 than I had in 2011, I was still pleasantly surprised by the scale of the reaction. I think it worked because of its simplicity, it was easy for anyone to get behind it. Each #FrásaAnLae now averages about forty likes and some are much more popular than others. But what they all have in common is they are free from any nagging or elitist Irish-language hang-ups.

The Irish Phrase of the Day is: bhí sé imithe, rud a
chuir lúcháir uirthi
Meaning: to her delight, he had gone
#FrásaAnLae #Gaeilge
10:01 PM • Sep 6, 2019
**20** Retweets                    **92** Likes

—

Today's Irish phrase of the day is: Is tóin tur tráite í
Meaning: She's an absolute dry-shite
#FrásaAnLae #Gaeilge
12:01 AM • Dec 20, 2018
**38** Retweets                    **178** Likes

—

Today's Irish phrase of the day is: Creideann sé
gurb as a tóin a dtagann an ghrian
Meaning: He thinks the sun shines out her arse
#FrásaAnLae #Gaeilge
12:04 AM • Dec 19, 2018
**34** Retweets                    **146** Likes

They are just entertaining phrases and there's no
slap on the wrist if you reply to me in English. I'm not
trying to police anyone's grammar because, as you will
know by now, that's not my cup of tea. What people
seem to love about #FrásaAnLae is that it's not afraid to
be crude, humorous or cheeky and you'll notice above
that the really popular ones seem to be the sweary ones.
Learning to swear in another language can often feel
like a breakthrough. The same can be said of learning

foreign-language jokes (and laughing at them). Vulgarity and humour can unlock a language and its psyche. I've seen through #FrásaAnLae just how rich and alive Irish is today and it's a beautiful thing to behold.

> Today's Irish phrase of the day is: tá cic maith sa tóin de dhíth air
> Meaning: he needs a good kick up the arse
> #FrásaAnLae #Gaeilge
> 2:47 AM • Dec 14, 2018
> **101** Retweets                    **425** Likes

That one was spectacularly popular! Clearly, these phrases ooze a humour you won't encounter in any other language. Moreover, I think another reason why #FrásaAnLae has worked is that it's a quick daily lesson that is much more relatable than any of the stock phrases we find in school books. It's 'do-it-yourself' Gaeilge at its finest with everything at your fingertips. Returning to my theme of language immersion, #FrásaAnLae succeeds as subtle and modern language learning. I've wanted to free Irish from An Caighdeán Oifigiúil (Official Standard) to remove its often negative connections with school. And it seems to be much more attractive to language enthusiasts to hear from an everyday Gaeilgeoir like me. In my ideal world everyone's Irish would be grammatically correct, and we would all have an *ard-chaighdeán* (high standard). But until then, I really do think the internet and social media have a huge role to play.

#FrásaAnLae has now simply become part of my daily routine and I still enjoy putting them together. It was also the inspiration for this book! Sitting down each week and thumbing through Irish books, dictionaries and news pieces for ideas has introduced me to so many phrases that I never came across in school. Seeing them make a stranger laugh or notice Irish in a new way is another simple way Irish has had a positive influence on my life Like #WeAreIrish did, helping others always feels good.

Finally, here are some of the most popular #FrásaAnLae since its inception. Long may it bring joy and *gáirsiúileacht* (bawdiness) to your daily Twitter feed.

Today's Irish phrase of the day is: a leithéid de sprionlóir!
Meaning: what a miserable bitch
#FrásaAnLae #Gaeilge
12:04 AM • Dec 13, 2018
**4** Retweets                    **62** Likes

—

Today's Irish Phrase of the Day: 'Gread leat, a leibide!'
Meaning: 'Get away, you eejit!'
#FrásaAnLae #Gaeilge
12:05 AM • Dec 23, 2018
**17** Retweets                    **89** Likes

—

The Irish Phrase of the Day is: d'fhan sé an oíche
ar fad ag buinneachántacht
Meaning: he stayed all night talking shite
#FrásaAnLae #Gaeilge
10:05 PM • Jul 28, 2019
**33** Retweets                    **130** Likes

—

The Irish Phrase of the Day is: tá sí chomh
confach le mála easóg inniu
Meaning: she's as cranky as a bag of weasels today
#FrásaAnLae #Gaeilge
10:00 PM • Jul 27, 2019
**47** Retweets                    **239** Likes

—

Today's Irish phrase of the day is: tá an iomarca
cáis ite agam ach ní féidir liom mé féin a stopadh
Meaning: I've eaten too much cheese but I can't help myself
#FrásaAnLae #Gaeilge
12:00 AM • Apr 20, 2019
**4** Retweets                    **285** Likes

# Tír Gan Teanga Tír Gan Anam

A country without a language is a country without a soul. When I think about Irish, how it's shaped my life and how my friends and other speakers use it, I think first about the positives. I can see myself using it to the end of my days and I see a bright future for the language. In that future, Gaeilge is allowed to grow and change. We can embrace the ability of Irish to adapt as quickly as any other language in finding ways of expressing new, exciting and relevant phenomenon. Irish words that look similar to their English meanings, like *pomagránait* (pomegranate) or *satailít* (satellite), show me that it's a beautiful thing when a language, especially a minority language like Irish, can 'make up' words to survive. And let's not forget how many English words borrow from Irish, some of my favourites of which are: brogue, colleen, galore and whiskey (but not craic!).

Similarly, while it's normal that we can't translate everything directly from Irish to English – there's no English word for *Gaeltacht* – I always find it interesting to try and create some fresh words from modern lingo. So, here are some of my Irish translations of recently emerged slang terms.

| | |
|---|---|
| woke (adj, awareness of social injustices, e.g., racism) | dúisithe |
| shook (adj, shocked or very surprised) | croite |
| mood (n, used to express the fact that something feels relatable; similar to saying 'same') | tiúin |
| thirsty (adj, libidinous) | macnasach |
| clapback (n, comeback or a sassy retort) | aisfhreagra |
| slay (v, nailed it, kicked ass or to look absolutely stunning) | sléacht |
| throwing shade (v, to disrespect someone subtly) | ag caitheamh scáth |
| GOAT (adj, Greatest Of All Time) | AFR (Ab Fhearr Riamh) |
| squad (n, your informal crew, posse or group of friends) | dream |

Since sharing these on Twitter in early 2019, they have gained over 1600 likes and nearly 450 retweets. With a little effort and humour, Irish can entice anyone, no matter what age they are or how 'woke' they feel.

With a pro-active and curious attitude to the Irish language it can remain an innate part of our heritage and community and can therefore overcome the doubters, the blockers and the elitists. Yes, I believe full immersion is the best way to achieve higher levels of fluency across the country, but I also believe in baby steps towards becoming an everyday Gaeilgeoir. Frankly, I have zero tolerance for language elitism (I have enough drama from the comment sections on Facebook, *go raibh maith agat*) so I've literally made it my business model to create accessible, fun and relatable Irish-language content wherever I go.

> *Don't take any shit from them*
> **Ná cuir suas le cacamas ar**
> **bith uathu**

Many times I have been watching, bucket of popcorn in hand, as cliquey Irish-language groups online go for each other about who isn't 'grammatically correct' or how there isn't enough 'proper' Irish being spoken. It's entertaining, but what a waste of time! Those so-called defenders of the language, who complain and give out, aren't doing tap for the survival of Irish. The ones who are ensuring the future of the language – regardless of their background or origin – are creating Irish-language videos on YouTube, or Vimeo, songs that hit the charts, translations and books that win prizes and become bestsellers, conversation circles where anyone can be heard, and safe spaces for debate and protest for Irish-language education reform or rights.

> *Actions speak louder than words:*
> **Ní briathar a dhearbhíos ach gníomh**

> *I have a real can-do attitude*
> **Tá meon an-dearfach agam**

I'm entirely convinced that positivity towards Gaeilge and immersion is on the rise. I see a swell of activity, where proud speakers of the language, of all levels, are coming together and raising the language's popularity. Demand for Gaelscoileanna, Gaelcholáistí and Coláiste Samhraidh is increasing; more and more parents can see the benefits of bilingualism from a young age. Over 26,000 people choose to go to the Gaeltacht each year and over 65,000 students in this country attend Gaelscoileanna, regardless of their level of ability, their socio-economic status, or their religious, cultural or linguistic background. They are no longer confined to the Gaeltacht; there is now at least one Gaelscoil in every county in Ireland with some of the highest numbers being in Dublin (40), Cork (30) and Antrim (13). When you see the joy on Irish college students' faces as they sing their hearts out in Irish, that's pure love of the language and a shared experience, one that no one can take away. Total immersion in any language works, as EF International and the EU's Erasmus program proves.

When I taught summers courses in Coláiste na bhFiann, new students arrived with little or no Irish. But in their first days we communicated with them in broken Irish to give them some time to get used to the sounds. 'Cad is ainm duit? Conas atá tú ag *feeling*?' With some gentle coaxing, a few words would be exchanged. We didn't *force* Gaeilge upon them instead we *brought* it out of them. Three weeks later, they had become con-fident communicators. We focussed on using Irish in a

fun and expressive way so that our students could interact with each other comfortably. This non-judgemental,
non-competitive and non-elitist way of helping students
to learn a language, at their own pace, was and still is
of the utmost importance to me. I was reminded of
Máistir Caball and the craic I had learning from him.
I was singing my heart out, learning without realising I
was learning. His teaching methods have stayed with me
for life. I see this approach to teaching the language as
a powerful way of encouraging Irish to flourish. Could
you imagine the fluency we might all enjoy after sixteen
or seventeen years of full and fun immersion?

Relevance and relatability are natural consequences of
immersion. In opting to absorb Irish into different aspects
of our lives, we can easily shake off the stigma and shame
left behind by our school experiences of it. I do things
with Irish on my platforms – Twitch, Twitter, YouTube,
whatever it may be – to show fans of the language how
to naturally converse on everyday topics, without fear of
making mistakes. I care passionately about finding ways
to make it easy to love and save Irish. The demand to
learn Irish is definitely there and I'm determined to help
others wherever I can. With over 11,000 followers on
Twitter, one simple hashtag like #Gaeilge or #FrásaAnLae
can reach nine or ten times that many people. Take, for
example, the time I asked my followers for their funniest
word as #Gaeilge:

**Catherine(Edel)Sligh**
@BlueLinnett
Replying to @unakavanagh
Bronntanas... it is silly but every time I hear it I see a big huge dinosaur walking towards me, poking its head around the corner of the sitting room on Christmas Day...

**ObstreperousLee**
@LiadanOConnor
Replying to @unakavanagh
Ag buaileadh craiceann - a far funner way to say having sex than gnéis ceapaim

**Faith Quille**
@faithwhelan
Replying to @unakavanagh
Uactarán (President/Head) because it always reminds me of uachtar reoite (Ice cream). Head Ice Cream : )

We live in a world of choice where we can learn any language and have resources right at our fingertips. I say ignore the naysayers who would prefer to deflect than solve or create. Naysaying is mean-spirited and unnecessary to those who genuinely love the language. I hope I've shown you how you can make Irish more a part of your life and shown that we need not confine ourselves to one language. What a great privilege that is!

My hope is that I give people real reasons to communicate in Irish. The approach to learning Irish in former days – by rote, memory and canon

– assumed that one size fits all. But in the Ireland of the twenty-first century, we all learn differently; some Irish-language learners will work well from grammar books, others will prefer flash cards, repetition and writing. Others still will prefer learning by podcast or by video. My greatest hope is for a balance of choice when it comes to learning Irish. My other hope is that we can all find a way to cut the Irish language some slack.

> This is only the start
> **Níl anseo ach an tús**

When I reflect on what I've done in my short life, I must acknowledge the fact that I would have had a completely different life and childhood had I not been adopted from Vietnam in 1991. I can't imagine a life without Irish and even though life at times has been challenging, I am entirely grateful to have had such a vibrant upbringing. I am a long way from the girl who played *Gardaí 'gus Gadaí* in the schoolyard, who used Irish oblivious to its far-reaching value. But growing up in Irish, with love for it in my heart and soul fostered by my grandad, is a privilege

I acknowledge every day in my work. And it was my mom who taught me and inspired me through her own work as a teacher that life is about making a difference and to always celebrate the diverse. Now immersed in the Irish-language community, I continue to learn from it every day. My identity as a proud Kerrywoman, a proud Gaeilgeoir and a proud Irishwoman grows stronger with each new connection I make. The diversity of my interactions with learners of Irish proves to me that it's as bold, energetic and alive as it ever was. Through the ups and downs, Irish has given me shelter. It's an innate part of me, it's mine to cherish, to use and to celebrate. Its future is bright. And it can be yours to love if you let it.

*Irish is a living language*
**Is teanga bheo í an Ghaeilge**

# Gaeilge is Your Superpower

Irish is a modern, fresh and evolving language and I want to get you using it every day. Once you've decided to give it a go, there are infinite ways to incorporate Irish into your daily routine. Here are some of my favourite ways to kick-start your journey to becoming an everyday Gaeilgeoir. These are all of twenty-first century relevance and range from the fun to the practical.

*Death Notices*
Listening to the death notices on the radio, particularly in rural Ireland, is an Irish institution. Around my part of the world, death notices are a primary topic of conversation, a bit of gossip to talk to the neighbours about and ironically they can bring life to a conversation. I know that jumping straight into listening to Raidió na Gaeltachta (RnaG) will be challenging, but – morbidity aside – the death notices on RnaG can play an essential role in your language learning. Consider this: they follow a pattern where the structure and the vocabulary are repeated with only the names and the

locations changing from notice to notice. This means you'll get consistent aural practice because the death notices appear every day on the Raidió na Gaeltachta local radio news segments at 8am, 9am, 12pm, 1pm, 4pm and 6pm.

*Email as Gaeilge*

Working in online media means I'm in my emails all day long so switching my Gmail to Irish wasn't a big deal, but you can go back and forth between the languages if you're unsure. Changing the language or your email account simply means labels, tabs, buttons and other apparatus (e.g., 'Inbox', 'Send', 'Reply', 'Move to' etc) will switch to that language. To find the Irish-language setting in Gmail, click the cog symbol (Settings) on the top right of your email account and go to the 'General' tab. Language is the first setting there and in the drop-down menu choose the 'Gaeilge' option. The next time you return to your Gmail homepage, it will appear in Irish. If you're using Microsoft Outlook, the process is similar. In the browser application for Outlook, click the cog on the top right navigation. Select 'View all Outlook settings' at the bottom of the list and then click, 'General' at the top of the left-hand navigation. From here, under 'Language and time' you can choose 'Gaeilge (Éire)' from the first drop-down menu.

### *Fócloir.ie*

This is the dictionary I use the most, in fact it's the one that helps me come up with ideas for #FrásaAnLae. The dictionary also contains sound files with Munster, Ulster and Connacht speakers. This is particularly useful for me because I've heard a mishmash of accents over the years and sometimes my brain forgets what the Munster way of saying something is! Entries are regularly updated to reflect things that are in the news (or just in the air!). I'm still waiting, however, for 'hangry' (when you're angry because you're hungry), 'FOMO' (Fear of Missing Out) and 'phubbing' (snubbing someone to pay attention to your phone instead)!

### *Get GIFfy*

Aodhán Ó Dea, Stiúrthóir Forbartha (Director of Development) of Conradh na Gaeilge was the first to show me that it was possible to create GIFs *as Gaeilge*. I, like millions out there, use GIFs (Graphics Interchange Format aka animated quick clips) every single day. First, download to your mobile phone a GIF creator (I use GIF Maker on iOS). Then, upload the media you want to use, still photos or videos, and then add some witty text to it before you save it to your phone. *Maith thú!* You made a GIF! Next you'll want to make your GIF available for others so upload it to the most popular GIF providers (e.g., Giphy.com or Tenor.com) and make sure to add 'Gaeilge' as a tag. Now if you search for 'Gaeilge' in GIFs on Twitter, you're guaranteed to see ones Aodhán and I have made earlier, like 'Slán Felicia!' for when you're not in the mood to deal with any drama and 'What the focal?'. It can take a few days for your GIF to appear on the internet but once it does, it's free to be used and shared by anyone.

## *Intros and Outros*

Simply open and close your emails in the Irish language, slipping in *a chara* after the name of your recipient (*Síle, a chara*), and experimenting with the different Irish-language sign-offs: *le dea-ghuí* (best wishes), *le meas* (with respect) or a *beir bua* (yours faithfully).

## *Nuacht1*

For people with busy lives, Nuacht1.com is essential. It's a website where all Irish-language news content is gathered into one place. It means I don't have to bounce between multiple news sites to know what's happening in the world. It's the perfect place to start your Irish-language media consumption.

## *Teanglann.ie*

After Dinneen's and Foclóir.ie, this is an essential Irish language resource which I've bookmarked on every browser and on my phone! It's a combination of Niall Ó Dónaill's *Foclóir Gaeilge-Béarla* (Oifig an tSoláthair, 1977) and Tomás De Bhaldraithe's *English-Irish Dictionary* (Oifig an tSoláthair, 1959). Both were Irish language lexicographers and followed in the footsteps of Dinneen. What I love about Teanglann is that apart from its large directory of words, it also has a grammar database which allows users to find grammatical information on rules affecting gender, inflected forms of nouns, tenses and forms of verbs.

### Téarma.ie

This was my go-to resource in college when I was writing up technical reports as well as my thesis on *tuairisceoireacht saoránach* (citizen journalism). The words on Téarma are more technical so it's a good resource if you're looking for academic, business or professional terminology. As a gamer this was especially useful as it's where I learned the Irish for boss fight (*comhrac fathaigh*), looting (*creachadóireacht*) and button mash (*scaollbhrúigh cnaipí*). Essential gaming terms, you'll agree!

### TG Lurgan

TG Lurgan is a music project by Coláiste Lurgan, an Irish college in Conamara. Their covers of huge hits such as 'Wake Me Up' by Avicii, 'Goodbyes' by Post Malone and Billie Eilish's 'When the Party's Over' gather millions of views on YouTube as soon as they are released. (I'm convinced that about a million of those views are mine because I listen to them nearly every day!) They also release their own creations and it's their modern approach to music that I believe captivates their audiences. They've inspired a generation of young Irish speakers to learn the *cúpla focal* and embrace music in the Irish language. I love their versions of Toto's 'Africa, Despacito' and Fun's 'Some Nights' because it's clear from the videos that the students are having an absolute ball!

*Use your Voice(mail)*

I've recorded my voicemail message in Irish using straightforward words followed by its equivalent in English. This is something that's quite common in other multilingual places like Quebec, Belgium and Switzerland. You don't need to worry if you fluff up the first take, you can just keep on recording it until you get it right.

> *Dia dhuit. Nílim ar fáil anois. Fág teachtaireacht le do thoil agus beidh mé ar ais chugat chomh luath is féidir / Hello. I'm not here right now. Please leave a message and I'll get back to you as soon as possible.*

## Paddy Kavanagh: An Appreciation

Very deep regret spread over a wide area when we learned of the passing of Paddy Kavanagh of Tralee, Co. Kerry on Sunday. Paddy, beloved husband of the late Winnie Kavanagh (née Vaughan), father of Breda and Noreen and the late Donal and Paudie.

He was born in Baile na nGall in 1915, in the 'fíor Gaeltacht' in West Kerry. His father moved from Muiríoch to Baile na nGall when he was appointed postman in 1908 and after his primary education Paddy joined the De La Salle Brothers in 1930, then returned home and joined the Garda Síochána in 1935.

After six months in the Garda Depot in Phoenix Park, he was sent to Glenbeigh to work where he met nurse Winifred who was based in Glenbeigh, 'my first and last love', Paddy would declare.

They were married in 1939 and their four children were born at home. In 1949, he was transferred to Tralee where he oversaw petty crime, a job to which he made an outstanding success.

He was affectionately known by his family and friends as a man of sterling qualities. He had many great friends in the moorland – people who were generous with their time and energy and people who shared their love and wisdom; most of these people are at rest.

He was a gardener with a great love of nature. In the moorland he loved nothing better than sitting on the *tortóg* [hummock] listening to the moorhen and smoking his pipe. The moorland was like Majorca at home to Paddy.

The traditions and attitudes that Paddy brought from his country upbringing made him who he was. It was his love of the simple things in life, the ability to meet his problems head on, and to have faith in God that made him a very positive influence on family and friends.

One of his best pieces of advice for success in life was to never to become so important that you take yourself too seriously. Through his practice of meditation, he nurtured his spiritual nature and the strong faith that he had been gifted with. His relationship with family and friends reflected the greatest commandment of all to him, 'love one another as I have loved you'.

To a dear friend we bid you a fond adieu.

# Acknowledgements

Thank you to the main woman in my life, my mom, Noreen, who had the courage to travel alone to Vietnam as a single woman and adopt a child who needed a loving home. I am incredibly lucky and grateful that you chose me! Thank you for always celebrating our amazing relationship, travelling with me and being my biggest supporter (even when I was being stubborn!). You are my inspiration. I wouldn't be the woman I am today without a mom like you.

Thank you to my godmother, Maria, who has always been generous with her time and hospitality. I have always felt so safe, loved and happy in your company. I wish everyone was as kind, joyful and as welcoming as you!

To my partner, Pádhraic, I would be so lost without you. Thank you so much for your love, geekiness and your ability to make me laugh when I need it most. You are my Player One.

Thank you to my best friends and 'Tralee Finers' Ciara and Lizzy. Ye know exactly why ye mean so much to me.

Massive thank you to Aoife K. Walsh, my superb and meticulous editor, who approached me in the first place about this book and believed in my ability to pull it together. I am honoured that you picked me and I am extremely grateful for how much time and work you spent on this with me. Thank you for your encouragement to keep going and keeping me on the right track. Go raibh míle maith agat!

Thank you to everyone at New Island Books for all their hard work on my behalf. I feel very lucky to have had so many people who were passionate and supportive about my writing.

Míle buíochas Garry Bannister who was generous with his time and enthusiasm for this book. I'm delighted that he was the one who looked over the many Irish language phrases throughout *Anseo!* His care and respect towards my work was very much appreciated.

Many thanks to Nguyet, without whom Mom wouldn't have been able to navigate the adoption papers in Vietnam. Her support and patience in guiding Mom through the process was invaluable.

Thank you to Ita and Dicky O'Hanrahan for welcoming me into their family and providing me with much-needed love and support over the years.

Táim ana-bhuíoch do Bharra Mac Aodha Bhuí ón Ghúm, a thug cead dom leathanaigh ó leabhair a bhí foilsithe ag an Ghúm a úsáid. Thank you to An Gúm who kindly let me reproduce a page from one of their books.

Go raibh maith agat Caoimhín de Barra agus Aodhán Ó Dea as ucht bhur gcomhairle 'gus oideachais maidir lenár dteanga álainn. Thank you Caoimhín and Aodhán for your advice and for educating me on so many brilliant aspects of the Irish language.

Thank you to Brian C. Mac Giolla Mhuire for taking the time out to chat to me about translating video games into the Irish language.

Derek O'Brien, thanks so much for being a punmaster. There's no way I could've come up with them myself or be as punny as you. Go raibh maith agat.

Many thanks to my cousin, David Kavanagh, without whom I wouldn't have been able to remember a lot of extra titbits about our grandad. Táimse ana-bhuíoch díot!

Go raibh maith agaibh muintir Scoil Mhic Easmainn. Thank you to the staff of my primary school in Tralee. I look back on my childhood with very fond memories and that's down to the teachers there.

Thank you to the people who are no longer with us but played loving parts in this memoir. Particularly in memory of Pepita Fitzgerald, who was so caring to both Mom and me. We miss you.

Agus mo sheanathair Pádraig Ó Ciobháin, gan

eisean ní bheadh an grá agam don Ghaelainn nó leabhar anso inniubh! Bhí dea-cháil air, bhí sé gradiaúil le gach duine 'gus ba shiamsóir den scoth é. Fear usual amach is amach a bhí ann. Braithim uaim go mór é gach lá. Ar dheis Dé go raibh a anam. Without my grandad I wouldn't have the love of Irish nor this book today! He was of great character, compassionate with everyone he met and a brilliant entertainer. He was a gentleman through and through. I miss him dearly every day.